BASICS OF
STRATEGIC
SOURCING

I0479764

SELVAN ATHISHTARAJ V

INDIA · SINGAPORE · MALAYSIA

Notion Press

Old No. 38, New No. 6
McNichols Road, Chetpet
Chennai - 600 031

First Published by Notion Press 2020
Copyright © Selvan Athishtaraj V 2020
All Rights Reserved.

ISBN 978-1-64850-975-9

DEDICATION

Dedication to my beloved parents

CONTENTS

PREFACE

It is a great privilege and an opportunity I have been waiting to share my experience of the last two decades' in procurement and sourcing. There is no hard and fast rule for strategic sourcing. This may depend on cost drivers, size of the industry, the volume of the procurement, type of the process and nature of the business and commodity deals. However, this would align in three major points 1. Market analysis 2. Spend Analysis 3. Negotiation. Strategic sourcing concept has been developed to increase the organization profitability through the effective procurement process.

This concept was developed in mid-1990 to avoid the misalignment in the supply chain operation towards the organisation objective and goals. The global markets are driven by the competitive advantages of the best quality and better price. These two are the pillars of any sourcing activities. This course and book have carefully written, and I have taken care of all the essential key elements of strategic sourcing of the present and the future.

In this book, I have given more importance to spend analysis and negotiation, which will go to the direct bottom line and business wining of order booking and profitability. Strategic sourcing is the systematic approach of selection and identification of sources. This is a continuous process and upgrading the benchmark to the next level or set up the standards to a new scale of measurement. In other words, do constant research and analytical process and keep away from regular procurement or day to day activities of buying. In general, this function will work as a separate cell or module and gives the inputs to the supply chain and materials function.

I have mentioned all types and patterns of each chapter described clearly to suit to industry, wherever applicable. These theories are only the guidelines and road map to adopt the sourcing and purchasing functions. Note that, adjustment, alteration and combinations are required according to the procurement type and industry business nature.

Selvan Athishtaraj V

07/03/2020

ACKNOWLEDGEMENTS

Before writing this book, I read and referred to many journals, reviews and great authors of sourcing and supply chain books. This book could not have been realized without the support and sharing of knowledge from my suppliers, people who kindly contributed their time, information, articles and book materials and reviews. I thank my old classmates in B-School, alumni at LIBA and friends in FMCG and Engineering industries.

1

SOURCING CONCEPT

The concept of sourcing was born in the 1800s at a time when it was a clerical operation and managing the records. The theme of sourcing was coined in 1832. The importance of purchase function was mentioned by Charles Babbage in his book *On the Economy of Machinery and Manufacturing*. Charles Babbage is also known as the first "Materials Man." Purchasing activity started on in early 1850 in a simple way of contract management in procurement activities. In the latter stage of 1866, manufacturing and the procurement need were evolved mainly due to faster growth in railroad industries in the United States. The purchasing issue was openly discussed in the book *The Handling of Railway Supplies* and their purchase disposition in 1887.

During early 1900, purchasing function was attached to various other departments like accounts, manufacturing and other functions expect railroad organisation. During World War I and II, the importance of purchasing function was rapidly increased mainly for raw material and sub-contracting activities for factories, railroads and mines. In the time between the 1950s and 1960s, the purchasing activity continued to gain stature as the technique for performing the function got more refined.

The scarcity of materials was the biggest challenge in World War I, and the demands were almost unlimited. The post-world war period saw a development of the value analysis techniques practised in the General Electric company in 1847. The design of this technique gave a greater impact on the reduction in overall product cost. Good visibility was seen in DMC (Direct material cost) reduction in manufacturing. From 1947–60, reforms activities took place in materials management sourcing, new thinking and practise placed in many industries to maximize the growth and meet the market demands. The period of 13 years (1947–60) saw actual development of purchasing and sourcing policy in many organisations in the extensive spread manner based on the needs and wants. This resulted in a dramatic growth in sourcing and procurement activities worldwide in many organisations. During this period, professional approaches evolved in purchasing function in systematic ways on their own framework. After World War II, the Vietnam War was given pressure and materials availability, and prices shot upwards to increase the focus on supply chain and materials management. People gave more importance to materials planning, inventory control, EOQ (economic ordering quantity) and MOQ (minimum ordering quantity) in procurement, stores control, quality control, cost control, material movement and surplus disposal.

In 1970 the oil embargo and the shortage of almost all the basic raw materials led to industries focusing on the purchasing arena with analytical and long-term approaches. After the 1970s, globalisation and global sourcing activities emerged. Materials management functions are centroid to cost-conscious, collaborative bargaining and negotiation, volume-based cost reduction. These are more dependent on the market scenario and in-line with supply and demand pattern. Materials management and purchasing the function data were done through electronic system devices in the 1960s. EDI (Electronic Data Exchange) was developed to maintain the database. At the initial stage of purchase and materials management, MRP/ERP system was implemented. This actually took place in the later stage of 1960. The MRP/ERP system was first introduced by George Plossl and Joseph Orlicky in the late 1960s. Oliver Wight contributed to the evolution of MRP II, to include more than the factory production and material needs. ERP evolved with the change in hardware/software capability and "Interface" interpretations between software

The period of 1980–90 saw many changes in the manufacturing approached. GE has played a vital role in the conceptual changes during the period. These are all continuous of Motorola Six Sigma and TPS (Toyota Production system). The basis of the development comes from Deming, Juran and Ohno (1950–70) inventors of the scientific manufacturing process. In the 1980s it started with JIT (Just In Time) kanbans, pull system and visual management. Later this reached lean production in the 1990s with value stream mapping, lean thinking and business process reengineering.

In 1990, this was further developed into a new type of programme, and it was called the ERP (Enterprise resource planning). Initial programmes were developed through FoxPro, GOBAL and went up to Java Oracle and .NET. JD EDWARDS, PEOPLE SOFT, SAP and many other packages were available in ERP for materials functions. This era has continued to develop into the 21st century with the expansion of Internet-based collaborative systems and E-Procurement.

In 1982 supply chain management and strategic sourcing gained great importance due to the evolution of many Japanese concepts like JIT (Just In Time) and pull-push concept. Feeding materials directly to the assembly line with zero inventory and zero waiting time was developed.

This was evaluated with basic planning, It started with demand plan activities. Forecast the requirement according to the market lead time to expedite the items through MRP.

What is MRP?

MRP, i.e., material requirement planning is a software-based production planning and inventory control system to manage the manufacturing function although it is not common nowadays.

Objective of MRP:

To plan the manufacturing activities, purchasing activities and delivery schedules.

To ensure the availability of materials and products for production and delivery to the customer.

To manage and maintain the lowest level of inventory with replenishment.

TYPES OF MRP

MRP is classified into three types (I, II and III)

MRP – Material Requirement Planning. This gives details of items required, quantity and time for in-house and suppliers to manufacture the product. It gives two types of output. (1) Recommended production schedule (2) recommended purchasing schedule. Both the schedules are in-line with MPS (Master Production Schedule)

Reports and messages:

1. Earliest start date and completion date

2. Planning schedules and routing

3. Purchase orders and delivery schedule

4. Reschedule – recommend for cancellation, increasing quantity, delaying or speeding up and advancing the existing orders

General MRP Data for Planning Process

The end item (final product) is created. This is sometimes called Independent Demand or Level "0" on BOM (Bill of materials).

How much is required at a time to manage the end item or next customer?

When are the quantities required to meet demand?

The shelf life of stored materials with expiry details.

Inventory status records. Pipeline, WIP and finished product.

Bills of materials. Details of the materials, components and subassemblies required to make each product.

Planning Data. This includes all the restraints and directions to produce the end items. This includes items such as: Routings, Manpower and Machine Hours Standards, Quality and Testing Standards, Pull/ Work Cell and Push commands, Lot sizing techniques (i.e. Fixed Lot Size, Lot-For-Lot, and Economic Order Quantity), nesting of raw material with reduced waste, invisible losses (burning losses and fusion) Scrap Percentages, and other inputs.

MRP II

MRP – I failed due to the lack of capacity calculation and demand forecast. MRP – II was implemented for capacity calculation of resources and predict the demand in the assembly and manufacturing process.

This is mainly to manage the fluctuating demand and forecast the change in demand. It provides a long-term perspective and better control for a healthy organization

This is a single flow of connection with marketing finance and other supporting functions. The plan is to create a work plan for 2 years, 3 years, and 5 years to calculate all the resources and capacity required for production and manufacturing. This will help us to predict things with a long-term goal in mind. This is a closed-loop system with feedback and performance monitoring. This can also be used for calculating vendor performance shop utilization and surge load management.

MRP II Reports

1. Item Master
2. Historical data
3. Master Production Schedule (MPS)
4. Production Resource Data (PRD)
5. Capacity Requirement Planning (CRP)
6. Shop Floor Control (SFC)
7. Material Requirement Planning (MRP)
8. Purchase Requisition (PR)
9. Work Order Generation (WO)
10. Distribution Resource Planning (DRP)
11. Standard costing and cost control
12. Moving Average Estimation
13. Lot Traceability
14. Finite Capacity Scheduling(FCS)
15. Blanket Estimation

MRP III

MPR III is a form of bandwidth management to take proactive measures to manage and operate the manufacturing process. In this, controls and indicators are put to know which is falling outside of the bandwidth to take the necessary action. This is a completely integrated order management system to view the availability to promise an ideal inventory. The total inbuilt reports can be taken from MRP III with the current order, existing backlog, WIP, FG and available inventory. This can be used for "Crash buy" and rescheduling, full shipment, partial shipment and short supply warranty and after-sales management. All the rest will be inclusive of MRP – II.

Today MRP has been replaced with customized Entrepreneur Resource Planning, and some companies use digital planning software with mobile applications.

2

EVOLVING OF
STRATEGIC SOURCING

The definition of sourcing is the processes involved in identifying potential vendors, conducting negotiations and engaging purchasing agreements to provide goods and/or services that meet procurement needs. In the course of time, the role and character of purchasing have constantly been changing. Traditionally, purchasing was seen as a merely supportive and supplementary operational activity, with little significance on a firm's performance. During the 1970's purchasing departments had a "more administrative than strategic" character. It used to be a department solely handling buying orders for other divisions with its main aim to achieve maximum price reductions. Even top management did not realize the importance of purchasing and its contribution to a firm's performance and regarded it as playing a passive role within the firm. Economic crisis such as the oil crisis in 1973 and subsequent supply disruptions supported the changing mind-set of managers. The management of external resources became increasingly important and thus, was ranked higher on a firm's agenda. During the 1980s, a connection between organizational strategy and a company's performance was established. A previously operational and unimportant activity was now recognized as being tactical. Purchasing became more and more integrated and covered the involvement of purchasing in the product, process, and supplier selection and contracting.

Supplier selection is one of the most critical activities for many companies, and the selection of the wrong supplier could be enough to dent the company's financial and operational position. Selection of a proper supplier which provides the company with the exact product/raw material and/or services at the right price at the right time and in the required quantities is very important Supplier sourcing is, therefore, a complex multi-objective and multi-attribute decision-making process. In the last decade; a lot of changes were seen in the supplier selection process. Many industries are now abandoning the lowest bidder supplier selection methodology of the past as a replacement for empowering multidisciplinary sourcing teams to select the best supplier available for each component. Sourcing by identifying and locating suppliers is relatively simple, but it becomes more complex as the amount of unique raw materials, ingredients, parts, components, connectors, apparatus, products, equipment, supplies, and services increase and the numbers of buyers involved in the decisions expand. The risks of buying the wrong items, services or from the wrong supplier can have major impacts and ripple throughout a business. Consequences can range from late delivery to total service failure liability and can even affect market competitiveness. In addition, if the selected suppliers cannot provide opportunities to reduce costs, improve and upgrade product/service offerings or provide other market-facing advantages, then an organization can quickly find itself losing market share.

Terms like purchasing, procurement and sourcing are often found to be used with the same meaning in discussions about the buying activities. However, the three of them have different meanings and different levels. Purchasing refers to the function of buying or acquiring goods and services as a transactional activity. It manages the flow of materials and information as an operational process, searching for the lower purchasing cost. This operational level includes placing purchase orders, expediting materials, monitoring the deliveries, and dealing with daily problems on the quality and quantity of the materials received, and evaluate the supplier's performance. The purchasing term is often interchanged with the procurement term. However, procurement involves additional activities to the purchasing transactions, such as the materials management including goods and services and secures that the purchasing activities achieve the appropriate service. This activity has a tactical level, and deals with the agreements with suppliers, conducting audits and certifications, a quality improvement on materials, and programs dedicated to the improvement on supplier's performance. On the other hand, sourcing concentrates in the development of supply channels in a strategic way, and it searches not only to the lowest purchasing cost but for the lowest total cost. It has a strategic level that covers the purchasing decisions on long-term and influences the organization's position in the industry. Some of these decisions include establishing long-term contracts, investment decisions, and sourcing strategies to use, such as where to source the materials. It is the joint effort of a cross-functional team that includes sourcing, procurement, engineering, quality, design, manufacturing, and logistics, among others. In essence, sourcing is where we set up the blueprint for our supply chain. Hence, it is possible to say that the purchasing activities are operational buying activities, procurement is the managerial and tactical activities that encompass purchasing activities and materials management. While the sourcing activities are strategic activities that search for the best supply solutions and feed the purchasing activities, and consequently the procurement activities as well. Even though there are differences among these terms, the literature mixes them, more often they use as synonyms the purchasing and procurement terms, some literature uses the term procurement to cover all the supplier-related activities including sourcing and purchasing. There will be a difference in meaning while using the terms sourcing and procurement, and the term procurement will encompass the new term of strategic sourcing.

STRATEGIC PURCHASING

The evolution of purchasing makes clear that conventional purchasing was intended to buy the materials of the right quality, in the right quantity, from the right source delivered to the right place at the right time at the right place. This approach, however, conveys a rather reactive strategy of purchasing where the focus is on transactions rather than on relations and also more on an operational or tactical level rather than on a strategic one. In our book strategic purchasing is defined as: The process of planning, implementing, evaluating and controlling strategic and operating purchasing decisions for directing all activities of the purchasing function towards opportunities consistent with the firm's capabilities to achieve long-term goals.

1950-1980	1980-1990	1990-present
Administrative/ Operational Purchasing	Tactical Purchasing	Strategic Purchasing

Truly effective supply chain management is planned and purposeful. A value-driven supply chain that is coupled to the strategic priorities of the firm is the result of deliberate management action and strategic corporate investments aimed to procure, develop and configure the appropriate resources, processes and metrics that define that firm's supply chain. A framework of supply chain design is proposed that comprehends three key levels of factors critical in understanding supply chain design: influencers, design decisions and building blocks. Influencers are higher-level considerations such as the business and political environment, the business model employed, the firm's desired outcomes and the supply chain life cycle. Design decisions include the social, behavioural and physical/structural design elements that define a supply chain. Building blocks include the inventory, transportation, capacity and technology decisions that are used to implement the supply chain. Supply chain design needs to comprehend these three levels of analysis.

3

SUPPLY MARKET

Strategic Purchasing comprises interactions with the supply markets to understand the current and potential situation and whether the organization is in a position to influence a supply market. This enables an organization to approach the supply market with a degree of confidence concerning real needs and the potential of suppliers in the supply market to provide the required item(s).

A **supply market analysis** provides inputs to strategic purchasing, identifying the organization's spend/risk position in a market, an indication of supplier's response to customer's positioning (Supplier Preference) and an analysis of vulnerabilities and risks in that market. Examples of non-procurement vulnerabilities to be analyzed as risks in the supply market are:

- Natural and man-made disasters and their potential effect on Supply Chains

- Trade influencing actions that are undertaken by governments

- The volatility of financial markets and exchange rates that can affect contracts and supplier viability

- Mergers and acquisitions across borders

- Raw material availability and

- Potential changes in global final product demand that may affect material and component availability

The supply market analysis will provide answers to likely questions in your organization, such as:

- What is the likely demand growth for the required product or service?

- Are there substitution possibilities or disruptive technologies likely to change the supply market demand?

- Is the number of potential suppliers in the supply market acceptable?

- How attractive are the potential suppliers in a closer business relationship?

- What is the production or service capacity currently available in the supply market from suitable suppliers?

- What share of the current capacity is controlled by the possible short-list of suppliers?

- How to map the knowledge of the product cost breakdown?

- To what extent can we support the potential supplier with the existing policy?

Supply market analysis involves the gathering of facts, data, observations and trends about the marketplace in which suppliers conduct business. An effective supply market analysis for a product or service starts with an overview of the global market. It is necessary to evaluate the major players in that market. Category Management is the set of business rules applied to define categories and sub-categories. Examples are within supply market groups – metals, ingredients, packaging etc. or within process groups – logistics services, travel and entertainment, facilities etc. The identification of categories will vary, depending on the organisation and industry.

Market Spend Analysis by category is to identify the structure of the expenditure, possible improvements in the buying process and most importantly, whether an organisation can exert leverage in that category's supply market.

DIMENSIONS OF MARKET

The following are the dimensions of market analysis:[4]

- Market size (current and future)
- Market trends
- Market growth rate
- Market profitability
- Industry cost structure
- Distribution channels
- Key success factors

Market analysis strives to determine the attractiveness of a market, currently and in the future. Organizations evaluate future attractiveness of a market by understanding evolving opportunities and threats as they relate to that organization's own strengths and weaknesses.

Organizations use these findings to guide the investment decisions they make to advance their success. The findings of a market analysis may motivate an organization to change various aspects of its investment strategy. Affected areas may include inventory levels, workforce expansion/contraction, facility expansion, purchases of capital equipment, and promotional activities.

Market Segmentation

Market segmentation is one of the important ways to find a competitive advantage with its differentiation in market analysis. This concentrates on market energy and power to gain a competitive advantage. In other words, market segmentation is the concept tool to get the force. In the market analysis, we need a lot of market knowledge to analyse the market structure and process. Segmentation needs a lot of market research so that we can get the information from it. Market segmentation recommends the market strategy. Market segmentation can identify customer needs and wants and develop products to satisfy them. It can identify different products for different groups, a better match between customer wants and product benefits, maximize the use of available resources, focus marketing expenditures and competitive advantages (There is no perfect way to segment market, but business can follow some rules like geographic, demographic, psychographic, and behavioural). Good market segmentation should be sustainable, accessible, actionable, measurable, and differentiable.

Element Market Size

The market size is defined through the market volume and the market potential. The market volume exhibits the totality of all realized sales volume of a special market. The volume is, therefore, dependent on the number of consumers and their ordinary demand. Furthermore, the market volume is either measured in quantities or qualities. The quantities can be given in technical terms, like GW for power capacities, or in numbers of items. Qualitative measuring mostly uses sales turnover as an indicator. That means that the market price and the quantity are taken into account. Besides the market volume, the market potential is of equal importance. It defines the upper limit of the total demand and takes potential clients into consideration. Although the market potential is rather fictitious, it offers good values of orientation. The relation of market volume to market potential provides information about the chances of market growth. The following are examples of information sources for determining market size:

- Government data
- Trade association data
- Financial data from major players
- Customer surveys

Market Trends

Market Trends are the upward or downward movement of a market, during a period of time. The market size is more difficult to estimate if one is starting with something completely new. In this case, you will have to derive the figures from the number of potential customers or customer segments.

Besides information about the target market, one also needs information about one's competitors, customers, products, etc. Lastly, you need to measure marketing effectiveness. A few techniques are:

- Customer analysis
- Choice modelling
- Competitor analysis
- Risk analysis
- Product research
- Advertising the research
- Marketing mix modelling
- Simulated test marketing

Changes in the market are important because they often are the source of new opportunities and threats. Moreover, they have the potential to dramatically affect the market size.

Examples include changes in economic, social, regulatory, legal, and political conditions and in available technology, price sensitivity, demand for variety and level of emphasis on service and support.

Market Growth Rate

A simple means of forecasting the market growth rate is to extrapolate historical data into the future. While this method may provide a first-order estimate, it does not predict important turning points. A better method is to study market trends and sales growth in complementary products. Such methods serve as leading indicators that are more accurate than simply extrapolating historical data.

Important inflexion points in the market growth rate can sometimes be predicted by constructing a product diffusion curve. The shape of the curve can be estimated by studying the characteristics of the adoption rate of a similar product in the past.

Ultimately, many markets mature and decline. Some leading indicators of a market's decline include market saturation, the emergence of substitute products, and/or the absence of growth drivers.

Market Profitability

While different organizations in a market will have different levels of profitability, they are all similar to different market conditions. This is a useful framework for evaluating the attractiveness of an industry or market. This framework, known as Porter five forces, the analysis identifies five factors that influence the market profitability:

- Buying power

- Supplying power

- Barriers to entry

- The threat of substitute products

- Rivalry among firms in the industry [citation needed]

Industry Cost Structure

The cost structure is important for identifying key factors for success. To this end, Porter's value chain model is useful for determining where the value is added and for isolating the costs.

The cost structure also is helpful for formulating strategies to develop a competitive advantage. For example, in some environments, the experience curve effect can be used to develop a cost advantage over competitors.

Distribution Channels

Examining the following aspects of the distribution system may help with a market analysis:

- Existing distribution channels – can be described by how direct they are with the customer

- Trends and emerging channels – new channels can offer the opportunity to develop a competitive advantage

- Channel power structure – for example, in the case of a product having little brand equity, retailers have negotiating power over manufacturers and can capture more margin

Success Factors

The key success factors are those elements that are necessary in order for the firm to achieve its marketing objectives. A few examples of such factors include:

- Access to essential unique resources

- Ability to achieve economies of scale

- Access to distribution channels
- Technological progress

It is important to consider that key success factors may change over time, especially as the product progresses through its life cycle.

ENVIRONMENTAL ANALYSIS

The environmental analysis can be divided into two parts: external and internal factors.

Political issues, potential social force and local economy are called external environmental factors. Internal environmental factors belong to the company's internal position such as employees, department structure, budget and so forth. How does environmental analysis affect markets? The government limits pollution emission, and they mention environmental taxes to block companies which produce substances that cause pollution. In other words, the government drives the organization. On the contrary, the cost of products increases due to environmental taxes. It means that the company may take the measure of reducing production, which may grow the unemployment rate by emission tax.

COMPETITIVE ANALYSIS

Competitive analysis is that company must know their competitors who have the same common services and products. The business can use like product cost, operational efficiency, brand recognition and market dimensions of market analysis.

The seven main dimensions of market analysis include market size, market growth rate, market profitability, industry cost structure, distribution channel, market trends and key success factor. There is another analysis of dimension market analysis. The dimension of market analysis can be divided into four parts; environmental analysis, competitive analysis, target audience analysis, and SWOT analysis. The market analysis is used to help the company to illustrate current trends in the market and how it may affect profitability. At the same time, market analysis is also to determine the attractiveness in the market. A good marketing analysis can easily improve organization investment decisions. It can be seen as a part of industry analysis by using global environmental analysis. The company can identify strengths, weakness, opportunities and threats so that the business can define the business strategy. The market analysis is also the reference for the company's activities, like decisions of inventory, purchase, workforce, facility expansion and many other aspects of the company. It has the potential to find the difference or competitive advantages between two similar companies. How can we find a competitive advantage?

SWOT ANALYSIS

Internal dimensions include organizational factors and also strengths and weaknesses. External dimensions include environmental factors as well as opportunities and threats. SWOT Analysis is a process that involves four areas into two dimensions. It has four components: Strengths, weaknesses, opportunities, threats. SWOT has been described as the tried-and-true tool of strategic analysis. SWOT analysis can be used in any decision-making situation when a desired end-result is defined. This analysis can also be used in creating a recommendation during a viability study/survey in the procurement strategy.

TARGET AUDIENCE ANALYSIS

For a company, targeting the audience means targeting their customer groups that are most likely to buy their products. The group can be classified with location, age, gender, income, ethnicity, and behaviour. And people who make a decision of purchase can also be divided into the target audience. Target audience is based on the spending group of three types: 1. Consumer market 2. Industrial market 3. Reseller market. The consumer market is purely dependent on the consuming pattern in that particular demography.

4

SOURCING PORTFOLIO

The technique (known as Kraljic) uses a matrix which analyses the supply base according to supplier risk factors: risk relates to exposure to supply failure and supply market complexity. This will be low in competitive markets for standardized products and services and high for specialized products and services unique to the purchasing organisation where there is a limited choice of available suppliers. The first portfolio matrix was described by Fisher in 1970 and later refined by Kraljic in 1983 and applied to procurement. Portfolio analysis is now widely used in identifying optimal strategies for category sourcing at global, regional or local levels, based on an assessment of two of the most critical factors affecting a supply market: Sourcing complexity or risk spend impact relative to the buying organization's total expenditure. By plotting these two elements in a matrix, an overall strategy can be determined and an action plan developed for each category of expenditure. Thus category management becomes proactive rather than reactive.

1. Profile the Category – understanding the category helps in understanding the collation of demand and usage information; critical, non-critical and bottleneck to understand the processes undertaken.

2. Supply Market Analysis – is including the identification of existing and potential new global and local suppliers. It involves a detailed review of cost drivers as well as the risks and opportunities available. It is usual to break down all costs such as raw material prices, labour, transportation, support, repair and supplier margins.

3. Develop the Strategy – cross-functionally determining where and what to buy while minimising risks and costs. This could reveal single or multiple, make or buy activities to meet demands over the term. It is important to ensure stakeholders are part of the full process, including the final strategy signoff.

4. Select the Strategic Sourcing Process – choosing and using the various tools and methodologies are primary here. From simple manual or electronic Enquiry and Quote forms to formal PQQ's, RFI's, RFQ's, RFP's and e-Auctions are utilised here. The documents, processes and tools used can be hugely complex, split into numerous lots. Key is to ensure suppliers understand requirements and price accordingly without it being overly onerous or lengthy. Product or service specifications, delivery and service requirements, pricing breakdown and legal and financial terms and conditions, as well as evaluation criteria, should be included here.

5. Negotiate and Select Suppliers – create a short-list, discard those that fail to meet relevant criteria. Undertake single or multiple clarifications and negotiation rounds with one or more suppliers. A final selection is usually done by the team and signed off as per the approval process.

6. Implement and Integrate – notify the successful suppliers and implement or fulfil demand over time or as required. Manage communication and changes with the supplier.

7. Benchmarking and Tracking Results – a key element of the sourcing management process. It is the start of a continuous cycle, starting with benchmarking the current status, monitoring the results and ensuring that the full value is being achieved. Go back to profile the category to review the supply market again and restart the process in a constantly evolving marketplace.

KRALJIC PORTFOLIO PURCHASING MODEL

The model involves four steps:

1. Purchase classification

2. Market analysis

3. Strategic positioning

4. Action planning

1. Purchase Classification

Start by classifying all of the commodities, components, products, and services to buy according to the supply risk and potential profit impact of each.

Supply risk is high when the item is a scarce raw material when its availability could be affected by government instability or natural disasters, when delivery logistics are difficult and could easily be disrupted, or when there are few suppliers.

Profit impact is high when the item adds significant value to the organization's output. This could be because it makes up a high proportion of the output (for example, raw fruit for a fruit juice maker) or because it has a high impact on quality (for example, the cloth used by a high-end clothing manufacturer).

Then mark each item in the appropriate place on the product purchasing classification matrix shown below:

Product Purchasing Classification Matrix

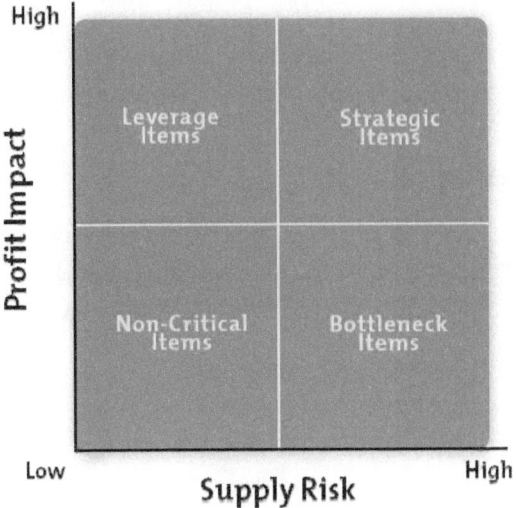

Strategic Items (high-profit impact, high supply risk).

These items deserve the most attention of the purchasing team. Options include developing long-term supply relationships, analysing and managing risks regularly, planning for contingencies and considering making the item in-house rather than buying it, if appropriate.

Leverage Items (high-profit impact, low supply risk).

Purchasing approaches to consider here include using the full purchasing power, substituting products or suppliers, and placing high-volume orders.

Bottleneck Items (low-profit impact, high supply risk).

Useful approaches here include over-ordering when the item is available (lack of reliable availability is one of the most common reasons that supply is unreliable) and looking for ways to control vendors.

Non-Critical Items (low-profit impact, low supply risk).

Purchasing approaches for these items include using standardized products, monitoring and/or optimizing order volume, and optimizing inventory levels.

2. Market Analysis

Investigate how much power suppliers have and how much buying power you have as their customer. A good way of doing this is to use **Porter's Five Forces analysis.**

3. Strategic Positioning

Classify the products or materials identified as "strategic" in step 1, according to the supplier and buyer power analysis, followed in step 2. To do this, simply enter each item in the purchasing portfolio matrix shown below.

Purchasing Portfolio Matrix

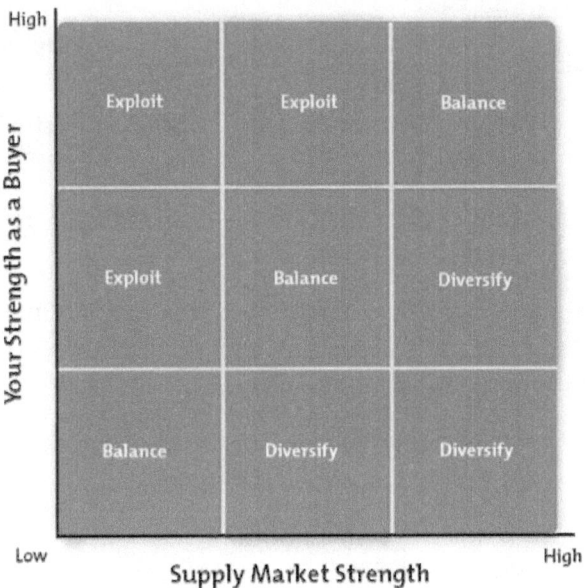

4. Action Plans

Finally, develop action plans for each of the products and materials are needed on a regular basis according to where those items are placed in the matrix.

PORTFOLIO MANAGEMENT
SOLUTIONS FOR SUPPLIERS

With Supplier Portfolio Management Solutions, supply chain managers can;

- Decrease expenditures

- Decrease commercial risks

- Reach new suppliers or evaluate potential suppliers

- Provide legislative harmonization

- Prepare top management reporting and other critical duties

Some of the services that can be accessed by portfolio management solutions are:

- Find the risk distribution of the list of suppliers in different industries and detailed analysis of riskiest suppliers

- Inform regularly about important developments in supplier portfolio and tendencies

- Measure the expenditure on suppliers by industries and dependency on these suppliers

- Check the possible risks and opportunities that can arise from this portfolio with the corporate family tree

ANALYZING THE PROCUREMENT PORTFOLIO AND DEVELOPING A PROCUREMENT PROFILE

The purpose of analysing the procurement portfolio is to develop a full and comprehensive picture (procurement profile) of the procurement needs of the organisation. The first step is to analyse the past and projected procurement expenditure or spend for goods, services and works (spend analysis). The next step is to analyze the difficulty and risk associated with securing these goods, services and works (risk analysis). The third step is to develop a procurement profile that identifies past and projected procurement expenditure and associated levels of risk in the form of a matrix. Finally, appropriate strategies can be developed for each of the categories of this procurement profile.

EXPENDITURE ANALYSIS

The first question to ask when preparing an expenditure analysis is whether historic spending data is a good indicator of future spends. To establish this, it is necessary to ask various questions, such as:

- Were there special events affecting the historic expenditure that will not be repeated, e.g. a natural disaster or large scale project that caused a large, but temporary increase in expenditure?

- Are there anticipated special events that will affect future spend, e.g. a forthcoming large scale project?

- Are there events happening in the external environment that are likely to affect the expenditure profile, e.g. political or economic changes in the programme country or in the behaviour of the donor community?

- Are there strategic organizational issues that are likely to affect the expenditure, e.g. changes in the funding profile or in the priorities of the organization?

If, as a result of this analysis the conclusion is the historic expenditure will provide a reasonably accurate prediction of future expenses, the next thing to do is to undertake an 'expenditure analysis.'

Analysing procurement expenditure provides data that can be used as a baseline to measure improvements, but also to provide reliable data for deciding strategies to realize short and long-term savings. Various tools are available to conduct an expenditure analysis. But first we have to download data from the financial management system, most usually the Accounts Payable. Data should include all invoices that have passed through the system within the specified time period. This data can then be analysed using parameters relevant for the particular organization, but typical parameters could include:

1. Expenditure and number of transactions per commodity or category

2. Number of suppliers per commodity or category

3. Average purchase order value

4. Total expenditure per supplier

5. Transaction distribution by currency range

6. Spending distribution between main clients

7. Spend and number of transactions per procurement officers

8. Number of procurement officers involved in the transaction per commodity group

SPECIAL FACTORS

While special factors may indicate that the historic expenditure analysis will not be a good predictor of future expense, in most circumstances, it would still be relevant to conduct an expenditure analysis and then adjust the results taking into consideration the special factors.

If there are factors involved that imply that the historic data does not provide any relevance in predicting future data, then the procurement profile would need to be constructed by analysing as much data as possible from information on the future strategies and activities of the organization such as project plans, budgets and so on.

The resulting procurement profile should provide as comprehensive a picture as possible of the actual procurement expense, including:

- What goods, services and works are purchased and how much is spent on them

- Comparison of historic spend on each item with the projected spend

- How the goods, services and works are purchased

- Who the goods, services and works are purchased from

- The geographical location of suppliers, e.g. local, regional, international

RISK ANALYSIS

Risk analysis should look at the following issues:

- How critical the goods, services or works are to the organization

- The difficulty and risk associated with securing the goods, services and works

The risk associated with each commodity or category is based on:

1. Risk specific to the goods, services or works

2. Organization related risk

3. Supplier-related risk

4. Market-related risk

When analysing supply risk, the following key risk factors need to be analysed for each commodity or category:

a. Nature of the supply market

b. Probability of supply failure

c. Strategic importance to the organization

d. Impact on the organization of supply failure

e. The complexity of the procurement relationship

PROCUREMENT PROFILE AND RELATED STRATEGIES

Based on the identified level of risk and the relative expenditure for each commodity or category of expense, the procurement portfolio can be plotted on a supply procurement matrix as follows:

Supply Procurement Matrix

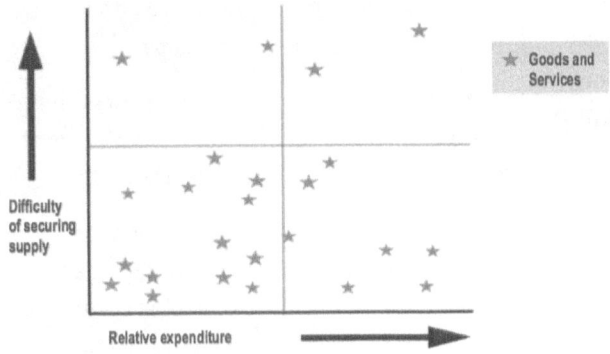

The diagram below shows the four categories of this procurement profile, including the main characteristics of each of these categories.

Strategies

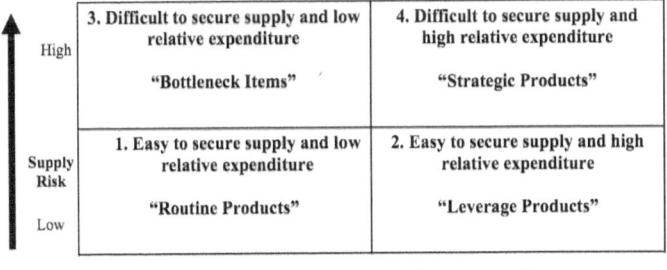

High	3. Difficult to secure supply and low relative expenditure "Bottleneck Items"	4. Difficult to secure supply and high relative expenditure "Strategic Products"
Supply Risk Low	1. Easy to secure supply and low relative expenditure "Routine Products"	2. Easy to secure supply and high relative expenditure "Leverage Products"

Low	Relative expenditure ($)	High

CHARACTERISTICS OF RISK LEVEL, SPEND CATEGORIES AND POSSIBLE STRATEGIES

The typical characteristics of each of these categories and possible strategies for dealing with them are highlighted in the table below:

Category	Typical Characteristics	Possible Strategies
Routine (Low risk and low spend)	Usually low-value and low volume items. Represent routine procurement processing. Typically represent up to 90% of the organization's suppliers. Often the suppliers are small businesses. Transaction costs can be greater than the value of the items themselves. Generally competitive local supply markets for these items.	Minimize administrative efforts by: Procurement at the lowest practical level (decentralized). Encouraging local suppliers to view the organization as a valuable client resulting in lower transaction costs. Focusing ordering and payment terms with suppliers on transaction efficiency (direct debiting, aggregation of orders, monthly accounts, payment cards, etc.).

Category	Typical Characteristics	Possible Strategies
Leverage (Low risk and high spend)	Commodities commonly used across the entire organization with high-volume. Represent commodities where there is potential for reduction of inventory management, handling and storage costs. Mature and competitive supply markets. Markets are served by a few suppliers with extensive distribution networks.	Total cost reduction and high service levels from suppliers by: Establishing automated supplier interfaces to minimize process-related costs for high-volume standard goods. Ensuring regular management information reports on the nature of this expenditure to keep a strategic focus. Establishing long-term agreements to simplify procurement, coupled with automated paying systems. Regionalising supply by using local suppliers that are agents for centralized arrangements. Forming collaborative initiatives with other organizations to build leverage, target off-peak periods in supply markets.

Continued…

Category	Typical Characteristics	Possible Strategies
Bottleneck (High risk and low spend)	Highly specialized goods, services or works.	Reduce the organization's market vulnerability and to secure ongoing supply by:
	Procurement is often undertaken by technical experts rather than procurement professionals.	Identifying alternative sources of supply and/or substitute goods or services.
		Holding extra stock where possible reduces risk.
	Technical specifications are inappropriately detailed and limit the supply base.	Developing supplier capabilities and/or changing demand requirements.
	Often there are only a few potential suppliers.	Ensuring long-term agreements may secure supply from key suppliers.
	Usually, there are only a few transactions in this category.	Encouraging new supply participants into the market;
		Considering local supplier development strategies.
		Developing contingency plans to deal with potential disruptions to supply.
		Developing performance or functional specifications to ensure a wider sourcing base.
		Developing a mixture of technical expertise and procurement skills to manage supply.

Category	Typical Characteristics	Possible Strategies
Strategic (High risk and high spend)	Represents goods, services or works that are critical to the organization. It is often a complex "bundle" or "package" of goods and associated services. Requires innovative solutions and high-level expertise from suppliers. The supplier's attitude to the organization (whether or not they consider the organization valued customers) had a high impact on the value and quality of the goods, services or works delivered. The category represents very few transactions, and there are often very few suppliers available. The costs in offering contracts are substantial for both the procuring organization and the supplier.	Manage relationship and performance through regimes and systems which are essential to secure value for money and reduce risk by: Encouraging effective supplier relationship management for complex and costly bundles of goods and services. The supplier's attitude has a huge impact on the value and the quality of the goods and services delivered. Maintaining regular communication with suppliers to ensure innovation and continuous service level improvements. Encouraging local suppliers with an incentive to deliver long-term value rather than suppliers for which the business is not significant. Helping to develop supplier's performance levels.

Continued…

Note: Procurement falling into the leverage, bottleneck and strategic categories would be considered "significant purchases."

5

SPEND MANAGEMENT

SPEND ANALYSIS

It is the process of collecting, cleansing, enriching, classifying and analyzing expenditure data with the purpose of reducing procurement costs, improving efficiency and monitoring compliance. It can also be leveraged in other areas of business, such as inventory management, contract management, complex sourcing, supplier management, budgeting, planning, and product development.

Spend analytics is one of the key tools that procurement organizations use to proactively identify savings opportunities, manage risks and optimize the organization's buying power. It is often regarded as the fundamental foundation of sourcing. It is a tool that sourcing executives can utilize to engineer superior performance. Data from spend analysis can improve visibility into corporate spend as well as drive performance improvement, contract compliance, and most importantly, cost savings.

Analysing procurement spend provides data that can be used as a baseline to measure improvements, and to also provide reliable data for deciding strategies to realize short and long-term savings. As procurement moves to a more strategic function in the company, spend analysis is its fundamental strategic technique which establishes a parallel process that guides senior leaders and budget holders in maximizing value for the organization's value.

4W3H

The process of spend analysis involves pulling together purchase history data to answer and assess the who, what, when, where, why, and how of an organization's expenditures.

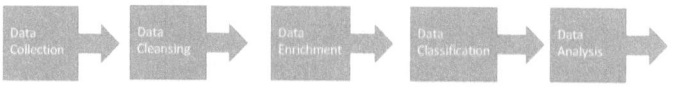

- Who procured it?

- What was procured?

- When and how often did we procure it?

- With whom did we procure it?

- How did we procure it?

- How much did we pay for it?

IDENTIFY DATA SOURCES

Sources of expenditure range across procurement of goods and services, employee salaries, rent, utilities, licences, advertising and marketing, insurance, training, etc. The sources of expenditure vary from business to business depending on the nature of the business, and hence it is an activity that every business must carry out uniquely for itself. Manufacturing organisations are involved in the procurement of input raw materials and assembly components and parts required for products from the various suppliers, both local and around the globe.

Although identification of sources of expenditure is necessary, plotting and identifying an exhaustive list of expenditure sources is a challenge in itself. Either an automated tool to collect relevant information at the source as well as eradicating the possibility of duplication or, in case of micro organizations, involving the heads of all spending departments can help overcome this challenge. A bird's-eye view into the spend infrastructure and direct material cost on product manufacturing should help to identify overlooked savings opportunities.

Data identification has to be done in the business unit, plant, purchase department, operation, marketing and finance.

Data Collection	Accept the available data Store big volume
Data Cleansing	Validation, Normalisation and Correction
Data Mapping	Classification and Enrichment
Data Modelling	Define, Integrate Multiple Data Structure
	Populate Model, Error Handling
	Rapid Development
	Repeatable

Data Analysis	Trend analysis
	Slice and Dice between dimensions
	Drill Down/Drill Up
	Graphical and statistical

DATA EXTRACTION

From the source of data, details have to be extracted in the desired format uniformly from all the data sources. Capture the spend data and consolidate all of it into one central database. Data is usually in different formats, different units of measurement and currencies. It has to be collected into one single form might be challenging. Tools are available to extract in uniform one single format to evaluate.

DATA CLEANSING

After the information has been collected and formatted, errors are then needed to be identified and corrected. Cleansing is about detecting inaccuracies and removing corrupt records and redundancies from a set of data. This can be removing duplicates, standardizing the name of the same suppliers to reduce variations, and correcting errors in descriptions as well as in transactions. After this process, the data should be precise and easy to read.

DATA ENRICHMENT

This is nothing but improving raw data with correct identification and codification. Data enrichment applies to the process of enhancing, refining, and improving raw data. It also includes standardizing the spend data for easy viewing. Enriching the data makes sure that all the header and line-level names and details are accurate and to a specific naming standard.

DATA CLASSIFICATION

1. Group

Grouping means combining purchases from the same suppliers together.

2. Categorise

After grouping, the data needs to be categorised by defining where the money is spent and what is being bought. In this part, the data is classified into multiple categories such as marketing, office supplies, software and legal. Identify how and where the business is spending its money. Unifying heterogeneous spend data into clearly defined categories makes them easier to address and manage across the whole organization. Classification is about harmonizing all purchasing transactions to a single taxonomy enabling customers to gain visibility to the global spending in order to make better sourcing decisions.

ANALYSE

Understand spend at a granular level so that the sourcing team can identify saving opportunities, granular enough to provide commodity level visibility. The data included in the spend analysis might include purchasing data, payment data, etc.

Procurement/strategic sourcing professionals are generally responsible for conducting spend analysis in the organization. The information is not only useful for sourcing professionals but also for management and budget owners.

Once the information has been collected, cleansed and grouped for easy reading, the changes can be compared to previous spending data, and it gives an opportunity to make new and meaningful changes. Identify opportunities for reducing the number of suppliers per category and negotiating better rates. The best probable method for cost savings can only be realized after the value on spend in the category is confirmed.

REPEAT

Data needs to be updated constantly to ensure the fulfilment of the contract terms and to keep up with the changes in the organisation's expenses.

SPEND CUBE

The spend cube is a unique way of taking a look at spend data because it is projected in a multidimensional cube. It refers to the three dimensions of the cube – Suppliers, Corporate business units and Category of the item. The dimensions could include sub-categories of the different units across the organization, from suppliers, categories, and cost centres.

The spend cube is typically the final output of the spend analysis process. It gives all the analysed data from a variety of angles. A spend cube is usually needed if an organisation has not managed the full percentage of expenditures across all business units.

The 3 axes represent Category (What we are buying), Cost Centre (Who we are buying it for) and Supplier (Who are we buying it from). These are the 3 legs of the stool – if any one leg is not there, the entire model falls apart.

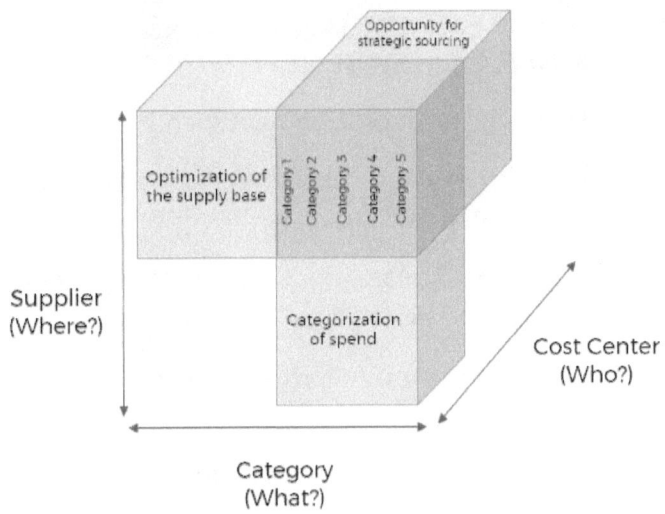

Each axis of this cube contributes critical information. Category analysis tells what specific types of goods and services we invested in. Cost centre analysis reveals who among the functions within the organizations drive the demand. It could also be the end-users. Supplier analysis tells which suppliers are getting the money today. One benefit is knowing if expenditures are scattered or cumulative, or if suppliers have simultaneous contracts in the organization.

Once all the data is collected, strategies can be formed easily. Slice and dice data to analyse it from many different directions. This data helps to decide which high spending end-users to align with, and which suppliers cost have to be targeted for renegotiation.

SPEND ANALYSIS OFFERS PROCUREMENT ORGANIZATIONS A NUMBER OF KEY BENEFITS

- Full visibility on procurement spend

- Identify savings opportunities and realize incremental savings

- Align and streamline procurement processes across business units

- Manage risk and maverick spending to ensure compliance

- Evaluate supplier performance for better relationship management

- Benchmark performance internally or with peers

- Data-driven strategic sourcing

There are many benefits of spend analysis. As per *APQC (American Productivity & Quality Centre)* – Best in class companies who have implemented spend analysis programs have lowered their cost of procurement because of cycle time reduction.

Total Cost of the Procurement Cycle as a Percentage of Revenue

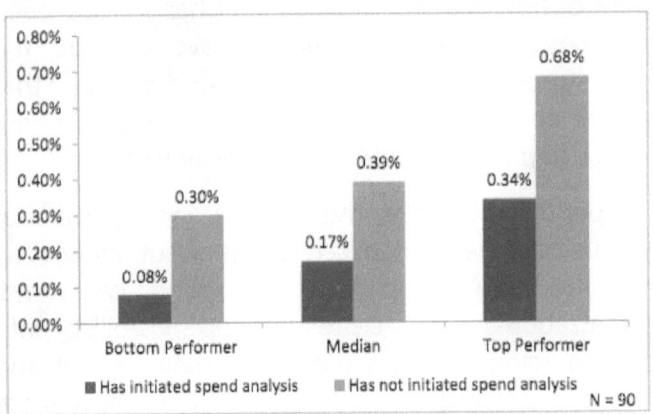

SPEND VISIBILITY

There are three core areas of spend analysis: visibility, analysis and process. Visibility in the spend management area refers to the ability of an organization to have a comprehensive view of the metrics that drive improved cost savings, process efficiency and supply chain performance. Having spend visibility gives way to the possibility of analyzing past expenses that can be utilized for planning future direction.

Spend visibility goes beyond tracking spending as it gives both a detailed and holistic picture of how money is moving through the organisation. Within the process of collating, cleansing, categorizing and analysing expenditure information, spend analysis provides consistent spend visibility information on suppliers, spend and compliance.

Without spend visibility—in this case, a real-time count of how much of their budget has already been spent—most companies would have ordered the office supplies anyway. They would find out later that they exceeded the budget for office supplies after the finance department publishes a quarterly report.

Spend visibility is the cornerstone of superior procurement performance. It brings about knowledge into the core components of spend categories. Organizations with clearer spend visibility into their sourcing activities can utilize their reports and insights more to drive performance and to make more informed business decisions. The real value is achieved only when visibility is gained into spend.

The macro-level visibility on the budget to the whole organisation and each department is to understand how much they are spending but also to understand where they are spending their money.

SPEND ANALYSIS BENEFITS

Comprehensive Visibility on Corporate Saving with Improved Data Quality

The key benefits that spend analysis can provide to an organization is heightened visibility and actionable spend intelligence. Spend analysis offers an organization greater transparency into the amount of money it spends purchasing materials and services. It allows the procurement organization to have a look into the core of their expenses and purchases. Data accuracy and consistency can only be achieved if organizations take full advantage of their spend analysis. Quality and depth of analysis improve over time. It not only gives them a more effective way to collect, store, and manage the enormous amount of data they have, but also provides a deeper understanding that can be used to develop initiatives and make confident spending decisions.

Identify Savings Opportunities and Realize Incremental Savings

In a sourcing function, the main reason to conduct a spend analysis is to meet cost reduction goals of the organization to improve the profitability and make the business more viable. When all the numbers have been crunched, the resulting metrics will show the spending patterns and the potential savings in several categories. Depending on the reports conducted, the organization will be able to cut costs through the use of alternative products, supplier consolidation and merging products that were purchased separately into contractible groups. Price reductions can be achieved through contract buying, improved contract compliance, and reductions in maverick spending. Organizations can also achieve additional savings on indirect items ranging from office supplies to temporary staffing, contractors and consulting services.

Streamline and Centralize Procurement Process and Other Administrative Efficiencies

Spend analysis has been proven to contribute to driving cost-effectiveness and process efficiency in a lot of organizations. The whole process will vastly improve, from financial reporting to budget preparation if there is detailed information organized around multiple dimensions. A more productive and efficient procurement function conducting spend analysis will build deeper relationships with fewer key suppliers and need fewer employees for unnecessary delegated tasks. There will be a significant reduction in cycle time for creating reports and ad-hoc analysis, therefore reducing labour costs or reassignment to more productive work.

Manage Risk and Maverick Spending to Ensure Compliance

When spend data is enriched with credit scores and other revenue information, it has better access to the overall supply chain failure risk of the organization. Good spend analysis data will allow to track and identify suppliers who have non-contracted spend as well as spend with non-contracted vendors. This could identify the categories of spend where there may be too many suppliers with no contract in place. The risk in the contract is reflected in the pricing, and that can be from a lack of orders being made or alternatively not being able to scale up fast enough to deliver the volume of goods and services required. The reduced contract risk to the vendor often translates into lower costs. Contract compliance information is crucial to being the bridge to savings. Enriching spend data with supplier risk information helps the organization in utilizing spend data to avoid supply chain disruptions.

Evaluate Supplier Performance for Better Relationship Management

The starting point for superior procurement performance and supplier relationships is information. Spend analysis provides insights and knowledge into their potential value for improved supplier relationships. Once the organization determines which suppliers offer the best value, it can work with them to establish more evolved procurement processes and inventory programs. Procurement professionals can peer into the performance of their suppliers to encourage proactive supplier development. At the same time, it can root out non-performing suppliers and help boost contract compliance by monitoring pricing on a continuous basis. Scorecards help evaluate suppliers and vendors by capturing metrics that evaluate performance. Having a comprehensive spend analysis gives more information on the amount of money an organization spends on purchasing materials and services, and for which suppliers it spends the most. This information is useful for contract negotiations and can be used to maximize the money the organization spends on procurement. If successfully implemented, this would leave an organization with fewer suppliers that it can work with to attain greater value from their suppliers and establish a more efficient and leaner procurement process.

Benchmark Internally

Having an expense analysis gives an opportunity to benchmark the performance internally across business units in different locations. It could measure how much is spent on office supplies globally. This paves the way to meaningful comparisons that can be used for strategic decision-making. Collecting and organizing spend data together in one place enables to list an average number of vendors or spend by category, and which vendors are generating the highest cumulative revenues. Understanding this is crucial to set targets for improvement that are realistic and achievable.

Leverage Spend Data Across Business Units

Data extracted and analysed in spend analysis systems play a major role in the strategic planning of the procurement function. However, other internal business units are also currently leveraging spend analysis to achieve their business objectives. The finance function can have leverage spend analysis in the vein of the procurement's main goal: gain a better understanding of corporate spend. Finance professionals can leverage spend analysis systems to analyze data from purchasing card, invoice, requisition or invoice sources as a means of generating more accurate accounting reports.

Work Collaboratively with Other Organizations

Each individual organization should develop their own blueprint to deliver savings and efficiencies, but working with a group can help generate a more powerful strategic plan. A collaborative spend analysis project will provide the group with the visibility to plan the most effective time to carry out a joint competitive solicitation for commonly procured goods or services. Having a firm understanding of which members of the group are buying those goods or services already can go a long way towards delivering savings and efficiencies for all involved. Having all spend data in a consolidated format makes it easier to get everything in one place. This generally has the effect of making collaborative efforts more strategic. This can easily identify common suppliers. It will then be easier to gain a better view of the opportunities. A collaborative spend analysis provides a proactive conversation and strategic discussion.

TYPES OF SPEND

The difference between direct and indirect spend often causes confusion. Let's review definitions and examples for both key areas of procurement.

Direct spend in procurement refers to goods and services that are directly related to making products. Examples may include raw materials, components, hardware and services related to manufacturing processes.

Indirect spend in procurement is the sourcing of goods and services not directly related to the manufacturing of products. Indirect procurement enables businesses to maintain and develop its operations. Examples of indirect spend categories include:

- marketing services (media buying, agency fees)
- professional services (consultancies, advisers)
- travel and lodging
- MRO (maintenance, repair and operations)
- information technology (hardware, software)
- HR-related services (recruitment, training)
- transportation and fleet management
- utilities (gas, electricity, water)

SPEND CATEGORIES IN PROCUREMENT

Both direct and indirect procurement spend can be grouped into categories, enabling analysis and management of similar goods or services.

A **spend category** is the logical grouping of similar expenditure items or services that have been clearly defined on an organizational level. For example, "information technology" may be considered a spend category covering both IT software and hardware.

The **spend taxonomy** is the way a procurement organisation classifies spend into hierarchies. One way to view spend categories is like a tree with many branches for different levels or sub-categories of spend. The number of levels in a spend taxonomy depends on the procurement organization's needs, ranging from three to six levels of categories and sub-categories.

Standard taxonomies such as the **UNSPSC** (United Nations Standard Products and Services Code) may be used to categorize procurement spend or as a starting point to create an organization-specific spend taxonomy.

TYPES OF SPEND ANALYSIS

Tail Spend Analysis

Tail spend is the expense in any organization that is not actively and strategically managed in all the spend categories. It is the place where procurement organizations may be leaving money and utilizing their resources inefficiently because it is usually least focused on. Though it is generally considered as low-value purchasing, as it contains a small portion of the expense (usually 10–20% under each spend category), it is a significantly important area of any organization's spend management. Because a large number of suppliers are accounted for, it has an impact on the company's financial performance.

With companies making millions of purchases every year, there are those that are too small or too infrequent and often get neglected. Procurement teams invest heavily in their core spend areas, but the tail-end remains a largely untapped opportunity for most companies. There is little understanding of how much money is involved in tail spend, and even lesser knowledge on how to manage it to realize the potential savings. This can lead to potentially losing millions of dollars annually.

Doing an in-depth spend analysis on tail spend helps encourage compliance and identify maverick spend, which refers to non-compliant transactions. The most common way of doing this is by carrying out a traditional spend analysis and then ranking the suppliers based on annual spend. The smaller suppliers that add up to around 20% of total spend are defined as the tail.

The figure above illustrates the simplest approach to analyzing a company's tail spend, which is by calculating the ratios of spend to suppliers at various points along the purchasing range. Here, the Y-Axis represents spend per supplier while the X-Axis represents the total supplier base, with suppliers ranked in descending order of size from left to right.

Tail-end spend management has been growing recognition and increasing importance within procurement. Putting a significant effort on it can not only yield potential savings but can also reduce costs and get more spend under management. The data compiled by The Hackett Group states that when tail spend is managed effectively, it can lead to 7.1% savings on average. When there is enough visibility into the tail spend, it is easier to identify areas that need to be sourced strategically. Segmenting the tail spend away from strategic sourcing managers and aligning dedicated resources with the right tools and capabilities are the best steps in managing tail spend.

Organizations successful at managing tail spend, segment the tail spend away from their strategic sourcing managers and align dedicated resources with the right incentives, capabilities and tools to attack the tail.

Vendor Spend Analysis

Vendor spend analysis is identifying how much of the expenditure comes from the critical vendors. It allows one to create a detailed spend profile for each vendor using historical consumption data. Knowing this can help one focus on getting the best value from these preferred vendors and consolidating the relationships.

A vendor type report collects spend based on the vendor and gives users the ability to select a comparable year and a review year. Spend data is optimized by identifying opportunities for consolidation and enhanced compliance. It helps visualize spend insights by the vendor, category, geography, etc. and enables multi-faceted analysis for data-driven decisions.

There are usually many low-value transactions with multiple vendors across many business units. The total number of one-off and small value vendors is usually big. Knowing this can help in streamlining and leveraging spend by identifying contract leakages and maverick spending. The aim is to reduce the number of vendors in each category.

Category Spend Analysis

The first step in doing a category spend analysis is to understand the scope and breadth of the category. Buying similar goods and services from too many different vendors? This analysis is built on hierarchies, and the spend transactions are categorized into the most appropriate category. The reporting allows one to explore the expenditure in the defined spend category hierarchy, which in turn allows us to identify spend leakage issues.

Allocating spend consistently into categories makes the data easier to navigate, interpret, and understand. When organizations can focus on prioritizing their top spend categories, it helps them identify and forecast savings opportunities. Prioritization will allow better negotiations for key spend categories to ensure more favourable contracts and pricing. By drilling into their spend data, procurement professionals are also gaining a deeper understanding of their spend categories.

When organisations have a high-level overview of spend by category, it is easier to identify categories that help in delivering savings and to realize which projects bring strategic importance to the organization. With this, we can easily figure out which action needs to be taken based on what gives the most impact on staff or operations and what the risks associated are. Access to detailed information on spend by category gives data to determine priorities and allocate resources in order to deliver the highest return on investment for the level of effort required.

Item Spend Analysis

Item spend analysis refers to analysing expenditure at an item/SKU level. It takes into account every individual purchase, classifying each one of them to identify what department it was for and what supplier was used. This analysis warrants the ability to know whether a specific item is being purchased from various suppliers or in several locations and with different item prices. Doing this analysis can highlight the different ways of purchasing in the business and potentially identify spend leakage issues such as purchasing from non-preferred vendors, maverick spending, etc.

Payment Term Spend Analysis

Payment spend analysis provides excellent insight for companies to analyze payment practices and terms within their P2P processes to identify issues such as unrealized discounts through late payments of invoices. It utilizes the data and gives a comprehensive view that enables one to identify unrealized interest from early payments of invoices. It explores the opportunities for leveraging all possible discounts or interest from the invoice payment process. It also covers the review of payment patterns. So a company can identify practices and activities that are not done properly

Contract Spend Analysis

This spend analysis tells companies if they are complying with their existing negotiated contract terms. It analyses spend with vendors by contract to identify spend leakage through non-compliant contracts. It ensures that the best contract deals per supplier have been negotiated and that all the buyers are purchasing from preferred suppliers.

Why Do Spend Analysis Projects Fail?

- Lack of Leadership
- Lack of Sponsorship
- Unrealistic Expectations/Unclear goals
- Data quality
- Wrong Tools
- Lack of Skills/Resource Support

FRAMEWORK – SPEND DATA LIST

1. The setting of realistic efficiency targets
2. Ability to capture savings

3. Workflow for realising savings potential

4. New comprehensive purchase programme

5. The business case for additional resources on an invest to save

6. View of local business and the potential procurement impact

7. An opportunity for improved budget management

8. The basis for a considered approach to E-Procurement

9. An opportunity for improved supplier database management

10. Reporting of meaningful data for collaborative purchasing possibilities

11. A model that can be refreshed in future years

SPEND ANALYSIS Vs SPEND VISIBILITY

Spend analysis is often viewed as part of a larger domain known as spend management. There are three core areas of spend analysis: visibility, analysis and process. Visibility in the spend management area refers to the ability of an organization to have a comprehensive view of the metrics that drive improved cost savings, process efficiency and supply chain performance. Having spend visibility gives way to the possibility of analyzing past spend that can be utilized for planning future direction.

Spend visibility goes beyond tracking spending as it gives both a detailed and holistic picture of how money is moving through. Within the process of collating, cleansing, categorizing and analyzing expenditure information, spend analysis provides consistent spend visibility information on suppliers, spend and compliance.

Without spend visibility, in this case, a real-time count of how much of their budget has already been spent, most companies would have ordered the office supplies anyway. They would find out later on that they exceeded the budget for office supplies after the finance publishes a quarterly report.

6

NEGOTIATION

Negotiation is one of the most common approaches used to make decisions and manage disputes. It is also the major building block for many other alternative dispute resolution procedures.

Negotiation is a dialogue between two or more people or parties intended to reach an understanding, resolve a point of difference, to gain an advantage in the outcome of dialogue, to produce an agreement upon courses of action, to bargain for individual or collective advantage, to craft outcomes to satisfy various interests of the parties involved in the negotiation process.

Successful negotiations generally result in some kind of exchange or promise being made by the negotiators to each other. The study of the subject is called negotiation theory. Professional negotiators are often specialized, such as union negotiators, leverage buyout negotiators, peace negotiators, hostage negotiators. They may even work under other titles such as diplomats, legislators or brokers.

The exchange may be tangible (such as money, a commitment of time or a particular behaviour) or intangible (such as an agreement to change an attitude or expectation or make an apology).

Negotiation is the principal way that people redefine an old relationship that is not working to their satisfaction or establish a new relationship where none existed before. Because negotiation is such a common problem-solving process, it is in everyone's interest to become familiar with negotiating dynamics and skills.

INTEGRATIVE NEGOTIATION

Inventive and cooperative negotiation based on the 'value creation' concept. It states that mutual problem-solving will yield considerable gains to each party. This is also called a win-win negotiation. Integrative negotiation is a strategy where the goal is a result that is as good as possible for both parties.

The idea of integrative negotiation is to work together to find the outcome that best helps both sides. This requires both sides to put more effort than usual into understanding what the other side requires and desires from a deal. Analysts of the tactic say it works best when the two sides concentrate primarily on the main point of the deal rather than coming up with many secondary points which they will then "trade-off" as part of the negotiating process. Integrative negotiation can be difficult, as it tends to require a considerable amount of compromise on both sides. Groups of people who are not used to working together may have to consider the negotiation to be more of a team effort rather than a competition. Although this can be difficult at first, many people who have experience with integrative negotiation find that it can work out to be beneficial for both sides.

SEGMENT NEGOTIATION

There are many different ways to segment negotiation to gain a greater understanding of the essential parts. One view of negotiation involves three basic elements: process, behaviour and substance. The process refers to how the parties negotiate: the context of the negotiations, the parties to the negotiations, the tactics used by the parties, and the sequence and stages in which all of these play out. Behaviour refers to the relationships among these parties, the communication between them and the styles they adopt. The substance refers to what the parties negotiate over: the agenda, the issues the options, and the agreement reached at the end.

DISTRIBUTIVE NEGOTIATION

This type of negotiation, parties compete over the distribution of a fixed pool of value. Here, any gain by one party represents a loss to the other. Also known as a zero-sum negotiation or win-lose negotiation. The single issue often involves price and frequently relates to the bargaining process. This is referred to as 'Win-Losese,' or 'Fixed-Pie' negotiation. These approaches involve the presupposition that negotiations are zero-sum transactions. In other words, negotiators look at negotiations as contests over a limited or fixed amount of some mutually desired benefit such that one person's gain is another person's loss. The totality of available benefits is often represented metaphorically as a 'pie.' Because the negotiators battle over a fixed amount of some good or benefit, negotiators hope to 'win' a portion or 'slice' of the pie at the expense of a corresponding loss (of pie) by the other (Fig 1). This approach is in contrast to approaches that seek to use negotiations as a way to enlarge the pie, or in other words, to multiply gains in order to make both parties better off (Fig 2). As a result, these approaches tend to invoke strategies that are distributive or predatorily in nature.

Fixed-PIE Expanding the PIE

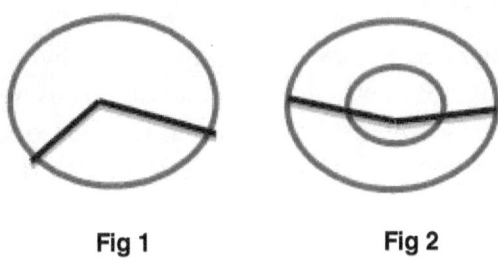

Fig 1   **Fig 2**

ELEMENTS OF NEGOTIATION

Negotiation comprises 4 elements: strategy, process, tools and tactics. The strategy comprises of the top-level goals – typically including relationship and the final outcome. Processes and tools include the steps that will be followed and the roles taken in both preparing for and negotiating with the other parties. Tactics include more detailed statements, actions and responses to others' statements and actions.

Skilled negotiators may use a variety of tactics ranging from negotiation hypnosis, to a straight forward presentation of demands or setting of preconditions to more deceptive approaches.

Coercion: using force, or the threat of force to wrestle concessions from an opponent.

Cherry Picking: starting out with a position that is higher than what we realistically estimate can be achieved.

Salami Tactics: prolonging a negotiation to a painstakingly slow pace, only giving a very small concession to the other side when it can no longer be avoided in order to placate the other side for a little while longer.

Bad Guy/Good Guy: Bad guy/good guy tactic is when one negotiator acts as a bad guy by using anger and threats. The other negotiator acts as a good guy by being considerate and understanding. The good guy blames the bad guy for all the difficulties while trying to get concessions and agreement from the opponent.

When a party pretends to negotiate, but secretly has no intention of compromising, the negotiator is considered to be negotiating in bad faith.

ZONE OF POSSIBLE AGREEMENT (ZOPA)

A "Zone of Possible Agreement" (ZOPA) exists if there is a potential agreement that would benefit both sides more than their alternative options do. It might almost sound like a foreign word for a cheer of joy or maybe even a new agreement of purchase. It's like a blue sky range where deals are made that both parties to a negotiation find acceptable. ZOPA determines whether there is a positive bargaining zone; each party must understand their bottom line or a worst-case price.

A ZOPA exists if there is an overlap between each party's reservation prices (bottom line). A negative bargaining zone is when there is no overlap. With a negative bargaining zone, both parties may walk away.

A negative bargaining zone can be overcome by "enlarging the pie." In integrative negotiations when dealing with a variety of issues and interests, parties that combine interests to create value reach a far more rewarding agreement. Behind every position, there are usually more common interests than conflicting ones.

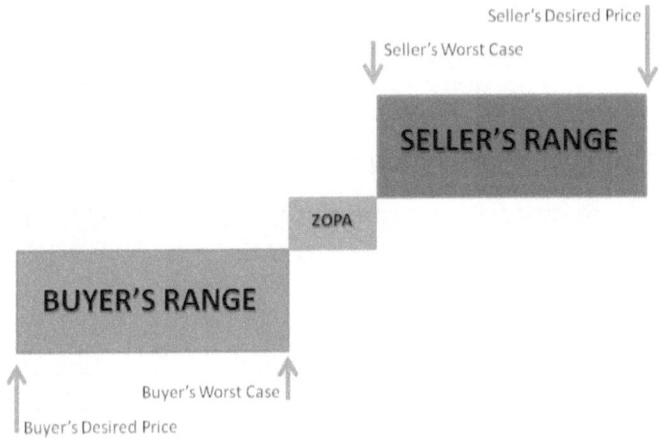

Reservation Point, Bottom Lines and ZOPAs

In any negotiation, each side has a reservation point, sometimes referred to as a '**bottom line.**' It is a point beyond which a person will not go and instead breaks off negotiations. It is also a point that is not generally known by opposing parties, and the value should be kept a secret.

Graphical Representation of ZOPA

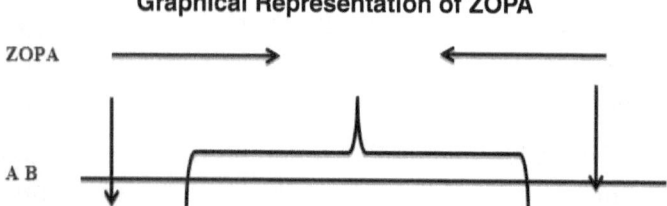

Point A Point B

When a ZOPA exists, there is a possibility that the parties may come to a mutually acceptable arrangement. Calculating where the ZOPA lies can be a difficult task given possible gaps in information, uncertainties about true values and the need for estimations. This is, however, a critical step if the negotiator is to have a clear view of the situation.

The process in finding this zone requires a little bit of detective work in order to make it work. It begins with a proposal by a person, commercial entity or organization known as a *'Proponent.'* Essentially, this is the person who puts an offer on the table. The receiving end of a proposal is known as a *'Prospect.'* This is the person or entity who considers the merits of the offer or proposal. The prospect will accept the proposal, make a counter proposal/offer, or outright reject it. This is where the game begins to get seriously fun.

The proponent is trying to sell us something. This can be a product, a business idea, services, and an organizational concept or a combination of these things. The proponent is more commonly called the 'seller.' The prospect, on the other hand, is more commonly called the 'buyer.'

The seller wants to get the maximum amount possible for their proposal. But generally may also set a limit for the least amount that they are willing to accept. The least amount they are willing to accept is known as the seller's 'Reservation Price.' This is the amount where they draw the line, also known as the 'walk away.'

The buyer, on the other hand, wants to pay the least amount possible but may consider a higher amount that they might be prepared to pay as well. The maximum amount they are prepared to pay is also known as the buyer's 'Reservation Price' or 'walk away.'

The differences between these respective lows and highs of both the seller and the buyer form their range of expectations. It has common ground or overlap between these two different ranges. This is known as **ZOPA** or the **Zone of Possible Agreement.**

S No	Distributive	Integrated
1	Zero-sum	Win/Win
2	Positional	Interest-Based
3	Competitive	Cooperative
4	Claiming Value	Creating Value
5	Conceal information or use it selectively or strategically	Free and open flow, share information openly

Continued...

S No	Distributive	Integrated
6	Make no effort to understand or use the information to gain the strategic advantage	Attempt to understand what the other side really wants and needs
7	Emphasis difference in goals, objective, interests	Emphasis common goals, objective, interests
8	Search the solution that meets own needs or block other from meeting	Search the solution that meets the need of both sides

NEGOTIATION APPROACH

Negotiation Theory

The fundamentals of negotiation theory are decision analysis, behavioural decision-making, Game Theory and negotiation analysis. Further classifications of theories are Structural Analysis, Strategic Analysis, Process Analysis, Integrative Analysis and Behavioural Analysis.

STRUCTURAL APPROACHES

Structural approaches to negotiations consider negotiated outcomes to be a function of the characteristics or structural features that define each particular negotiation. These characteristics may include features such as the number of parties and issues involved in the negotiation, and the composition of monolithic or comprise many groups or relative power of the competing parties. Structural approaches to negotiation find "explanations of outcomes in patterns of relationships between parties or their goals." They can be deterministic in that they often view outcomes as a priori once structural factors are understood.

In structural approaches to negotiation theory, analysts tend to define negotiations as conflict scenarios between opponents who maintain incompatible goals. Analysts who adopt a structural approach to the study of negotiations share an emphasis on the means that the parties bring to a negotiation. One of the main theoretical contributions derived from the structural approach is the theory that power is the central determining factor in negotiations. In this view, the relative power of each party affects their ability to secure their individual goals through negotiations. Structural theories offer varying definitions of power. For example, power is sometimes defined as the ability to win or alternatively, as the possession of 'strength' or 'resources.'

STRUCTURAL ANALYSIS

Structural Analysis considers this process to be a power game. The strategic analysis thinks of it as a repetition of games (Game Theory). Integrative Analysis prefers the more intuitive notion of process in which negotiations undergo successive stages, e.g. pre-negotiation, stalemate, settlement.

Structural Analysis is based on a distribution of empowering elements among two negotiating parties. Structural theory moves away from traditional realist notions of power in that it does not only consider power to be a possession, manifested for example in economic or military resources, but also thinks of power as a relation.

Based on the distribution of elements, in the structural analysis, we find either power-symmetry between equally strong parties or power-asymmetry between a stronger and a weaker party. All elements from which the respective parties can draw power constitute structure. They may be of material nature, or of social nature.

These instrumental elements of power are either defined as parties' relative position or as their relative ability to make their options prevail. Structural analysis is easy to criticise because it predicts that the strongest will always win. This, however, does not always hold true.

STRATEGIC ANALYSIS

According to structural analysis, negotiations can, therefore, be described with matrixes, such as the Prisoner's Dilemma, a concept taken from Game Theory. Another common game is the Chicken Dilemma.

Game theory uses formal mathematical models to describe, recommend or predict the actions that the parties will take in order to maximize their own gains when the consequences of any action they choose will depend on the decisions made by another actor. It is concerned with "games of 'strategy,' in contrast with games of skill or games of chance – in which the best course of action for each participant depends on what he expects the other participants to do" Games are frequently represented as matrixes or trees where each player must choose between a finite number of possible "moves," each with known pay-offs.

Another strategic theory is Critical Risk Theory of crisis bargaining. Like Game Theory, Critical Risk Theory uses cardinal utility numbers to explain decision-making behaviour. But it introduces the notion that parties use probability estimates when making rational calculations of whether or not to concede or to stand firm in crisis negotiation. These probabilities are derived from each player's calculus of their own critical risk, or the maximum risk of a breakdown in negotiations that the player is willing to tolerate in order to stand firm, combined with each player's estimation of the level of their opponent's inherent resolve to stand firm.

One of the best-known games to treat negotiations is the **Prisoner's Dilemma Game (PD).** This game reflects the following scenario. Two prisoners are awaiting trial for a crime they committed. Each must decide between two courses of action: confess or not. If neither person confesses, in other words, they cooperate with each other; each prisoner will have to serve a prison term of two years. On the other hand, if both prisoners chose to 'defect' and turn evidence against one another, both prisoners will be faced with a four-year prison term.

If the game ended here cooperation by the two prisoners would be likely, but in the classic version of the PD game, there is another set of alternatives. The prisoners learn that if one party cooperates and the other defects, the one who defects will not serve time, leaving the one who refused to testify against his partner to serve the full five-year sentence. Because each player is seeking to maximize his own outcomes, and neither knows what the other will do, the PD game demonstrates that the rational player will choose defection every time because he realizes that by choosing to defect he will fare better in the game, no matter what his opponent does. Figure 3 below provides a graphical representation of the PD game.

	A	COOPORATE	DEFECT
	Cooperate	2YEARS/2YEARS	5YEARS/0 YEARS
B	DEFECT	0 YEARS/5YEARS	4YEARS/4YEARS

The parties have contradicting incentives to cooperate or defect. If one party cooperates or makes a concession and the other does not, the defecting party might relatively gain more.

Trust may be built only in repetitive games through the emergence of reliable patterns of behaviour such as **tit-for-tat.**

PROCESS ANALYSIS

Process analysis is the theory closest to haggling. Parties start from two points and converge through a series of concessions. As in strategic analysis, both sides have a veto (e.g. sell, not sell; pay, not pay). Process analysis also features structural assumptions, because one side may be weaker or stronger (e.g. more eager to sell, not willing to pay a certain price). Process Analysis focuses on the study of the dynamics of processes.

The process of negotiation, therefore, is considered to unfold between fixed points: the starting point of discord, the endpoint of convergence. The so-called security point is the result of optional withdrawal is also taken into account.

Another important contribution to come from the behavioural approach is the work on framing. Frames refer to the way a problem is described or perceived. Influence is the emotional response an individual has to a statement of fact of a problem.

BEHAVIOURAL ANALYSIS

This emphasizes the role that the negotiator's personalities or individual characteristics play in determining the course and outcome of negotiated agreements. Behavioural theories may explain negotiations as interactions between personality 'types' that often take the form of dichotomies, such as shopkeepers and warriors or 'hardliners' and 'soft liners' where negotiators are portrayed either as ruthlessly battling for all or diplomatically conceding to another party's demands for the sake of maintaining peace.

Negotiations often viewed as either:

a. "Hard"

    1. Participants are adversaries

    2. Goal is victory

    3. Demand concessions as a condition of the relationship

    4. Distrust others search for the single answer: the one will get accepted

    5. Try to win a contest of wills

    6. Apply pressure

b. "Soft"

    1. Participants are friends

    2. Goal is agreement

    3. Make concessions to cultivate the relationship

    4. Be soft on the people and the problem

    5. Trust others

    6. Change the position easily

    7. Make offers

    8. Search for the single answer: the one they will accept

    9. Insist on agreement

    10. Try to avoid contest of will

    11. Yield to pressure

The tension that arises between these two analyses forms a paradox that has been termed the **"Toughness Dilemma"** or the **"Negotiator's Dilemma."**

The dilemma states that though negotiators who are 'tough' during negotiation are more likely to gain more of their demands in a negotiated solution, the trade-off is that in adopting this stance, they are less likely to conclude an agreement at all.

The behavioural approach derives from psychological and experimental traditions but also from centuries-old diplomatic treaties. These traditions share the perspective that negotiations – whether between nations, employers and unions or neighbours are ultimately about the individuals involved.

This may emphasize the role played by 'arts' of persuasion, attitudes, trust, perception (or misperception), individual motivation and personality in negotiated outcomes. Other researchers from the behavioural school have emphasized factors such as relationships, culture, norms, skill, attitudes, expectations and trust.

Behavioural analysis and approaches are articulated with four distinct orientations or 'types' of personal motivation formed by an individual's standing across two dimensions: the degree of interest in interpersonal relationships and degree of interest in outcomes. The resulting typologies of motivational orientation are represented as continuums: the individualistic, the altruistic, the cooperative and the competitive. A person exhibiting an individualistic orientation is motivated by an exclusive concern for his or her own outcomes. One who is altruistic displays an orientation characterized by an exclusive concern for the well-being (outcomes) of other parties. A person with a cooperative motivational style is oriented towards concern for the well-being (outcomes) of both parties. While the competitively-oriented individual is one, who is driven by a desire to out-do his or her opponent.

INTEGRATIVE ANALYSIS

The integrative analysis divides the process into successive stages, rather than talking about fixed points. It extends the analysis to pre-negotiations stages in which parties make first contacts. The outcome is explained as the performance of the actors at different stages. Stages may include pre-negotiations, finding a formula of distribution, crest behaviour and settlement.

Timing is considered to be another important factor in negotiations. Both the parties are unlikely to enter into talks before the situation is 'ripe for a solution,' a condition that occurs when the parties realize that the status quo "is a lose-lose situation, not a win-lose situation." However, the negotiator maintains that ripeness, while necessary, is not a sufficient condition for successful negotiations. For this, the presence of a Mutually Hurting Stalemate is also required, a condition of intolerable 'hurting' or mutual loss. This kind of stalemate arises out of the suffering that results when parties fail to solve an important problem. In general, parties enter into negotiations to escape an unpleasant state of affairs when they believe that in doing so, they have a better chance of achieving a favourable outcome, than by any other means.

BAD FAITH NEGOTIATION

Bad faith is a concept in negotiation theory whereby parties pretend to reason to reach a settlement, but have no intention to do so. For example, one political party may pretend to negotiate with no intention to compromise just for the sake of political effect.

Approaches	Basic Features	Assumption	Limitations
Structural	Focus on means, Position and power	Win-lose	Lock into positions might lead to lost opportunity for mutually beneficial agreement Over-emphasis on Power
Strategic	Focus on ends, rationality Positions	Win-Lose	Excludes use of power, players undifferentiated
Behavioural	Focus on personality traits	Win-Lose	Emphasis on positions
Concession Exchange	Focus on concession making behaviour, positions	Win-Lose	Emphasis on positions Lack of predictiveness

Continued…

Approaches	Basic Features	Assumption	Limitations
Integrative	Focus on the problem solving, creating value, communicating, Win-win solutions	Win-Win	Parties should still recognize and be prepared for encounters with no integrative bargains Time-consuming

ELEMENTS OF NEGOTIATION

Negotiation Styles

Five styles of Negotiation: Individuals can often have strong dispositions towards numerous styles; the style used during a negotiation depends on the context and the interests of the other party, among other factors.

1. Accommodating: Individuals who enjoy solving the other party's problems and preserving personal relationships. Accommodators are sensitive to the emotional states, body language, and verbal signals of the other parties. They can, however, feel taken advantage of in situations when the other party places little emphasis on the relationship.

2. Avoiding: Individuals who do not like to negotiate and don't do it unless warranted. When negotiating, avoiders tend to defer and dodge the confrontational aspects of negotiating. However, they may be perceived as tactful and diplomatic.

3. Collaborating: Individuals who enjoy negotiations that involve solving tough problems in creative ways. Collaborators are good at using negotiations to understand the concerns and interests of the other parties. They can, however, create problems by transforming simple situations into more complex ones.

4. Competing: Individuals who enjoy negotiations because they present an opportunity to win something. Competitive negotiators have strong instincts for all aspects of negotiating and are often strategic. Because their style can dominate the bargaining process, competitive negotiators often neglect the importance of relationships.

5. Compromising: Individuals who are eager to close the deal by doing what is fair and equal for all parties involved in the negotiation. Compromisers can be useful when there is limited time to complete the deal. However, compromisers often unnecessarily rush the negotiation process and make concessions too quickly.

Seven Elements

1. Interests

2. Options

3. Alternatives

4. Legitimacy

5. Communication

6. Relationship

7. Commitment

Interests

The first step of a principled negotiation is to understand that both sides have a certain set of interests, which is why both sides of the negotiating table interests are not the same as the positions or demands that people typically stake out and argue for in negotiation. A position is a proposed outcome that represents merely one way among many that issues might be resolved and interests met. The notion of interests encompasses a wide range of possibilities, from substantive goals such as money, deadlines, or guarantees to emotional desires such as respect, recognition, and feeling fairly treated, or even seeing another person happy. Often we have multiple interests at stake in a negotiation, some of which may be inconsistent and require setting priorities.

More generally, we want certain things in the short term but also want to maintain leverage for future negotiations (by not expending all of our bargaining chips now) and at the same time not to upset the rules of the game that we rely on (such as no one resorting to violence), even if breaking the rules might improve our immediate return. Much of the challenge of negotiation is in figuring out how best to reconcile such conflicts or whether there are creative solutions that avoid our having to make such tough choices.

Between the parties, interests can be shared (neither of us wants to spend too much time negotiating; both of us want to set a good precedent), differing (care about net present value, and care about cash flow), or conflicting (price, credit, ownership, who gets the corner office). While negotiation is often assumed to be an adversarial battle focused on conflicting interests, this assumption overlooks two important points. First, some of the most intense conflicts are often fuelled by identical interests— both parties want to be treated fairly. Negotiators are often shocked to discover this, which usually leads them to explore why their perceptions of fairness differ. Second, the potential value inherent in shared or differing interests may be as large as or larger than the value in dispute. In commercial litigation, for example, the parties' anger about something that had happened in the past caused them not to realize that, as circumstances had developed, the potential value of a continuing relationship was more than ten times greater than the amount in dispute. When an outsider pointed this out, the parties suddenly found the motivation to find a settlement.

Options

Although we may have a preferred solution, there are likely a number of different outcomes that will work for it and for the other side. Find as many of them as possible and figure out which outcome is best. Remember to look at them from the other side's perspective to make sure that they are suitable. Creativity is a useful skill in finding additional options in a negotiation.

Alternatives

In order to set realistic goals, negotiators must start by considering certain fundamental questions: Where will each side be if no agreement is reached?

What alternative solutions are available for meeting the goals? As seen earlier, attention to alternatives is an important feature of distributive as well as of integrative-based approaches. However, in contrast to the emphasis that is placed on concepts such as reservation points and bottom lines in positional approaches to bargaining, integrative approaches tend to take a slightly more nuanced view of the role of alternatives.

In negotiation, it is crucial for both parties to know their Best Alternative to a Negotiated Agreement (BATNA) both before and throughout all stages of negotiation. According to this principle, having a resolute bottom line can come at high costs. By its nature, a bottom line can be inflexible and onerous. It can prevent creative thinking and lock parties into positions that may prevent them from coming to a favourable solution.

A BATNA provides negotiators with a measure of flexibility that is lacking from a bottom line. BATNA's change when negotiators perceive a change in their alternatives. When negotiations are viewed in terms of BATNAs as opposed to positions or bottom lines, the negotiation can continue even when figures are rejected because negotiators are freer to continue to explore additional possible solutions. Moreover, because negotiation is viewed as a joint decision-making process in the integrative approach, there is always a possibility of either side reconsidering their position in mid-stream and deciding to pursue a different course than originally planned. Negotiators who fail to evaluate their alternatives to an agreement both before and during the process may therefore also be in danger of rushing to an agreement without having fully considered their or the other party's alternatives, leading one side to end up with a deal that should have been rejected.

BATNAs can be an important source of power or strength in a negotiation. A more 'powerful' party with a weaker BATNA will need to come to a negotiated agreement more than its rival. For this reason, Fisher and Ury maintain that developing a BATNA can be the best tool when facing powerful negotiators. In agricultural trade negotiations, having alternative trading partners, for example, multiple potential buyers for a stock of wheat who may be willing to incorporate side agreements into the primary purchase agreement, strengthens the seller's BATNA vis-à-vis, other potential buyers. Negotiators need to assess and develop their BATNAs before and during a negotiation. To do so, parties begin by making a list of the alternatives available if an agreement is not reached. Negotiators should also take the time to understand and anticipate the BATNAs of the other side, consider the options available given the two sets of BATNAs, develop a plan for implementing them and then choose the best of these developed alternatives. Knowing BATNA provides with "a measure for agreements that will protect against both accepting an agreement it should reject and rejecting an agreement it should accept." In short, it is good to consider the line of limitations beforehand. But a good negotiator will not let his limitations inhibit his imagination and the ability to recognize fruitful opportunities.

Legitimacy

Success in negotiation depends, to a large extent, on the ability to persuade the other side, at least to some extent. One way to do this is to have legitimate standards that it can be used to show the other party if it is reasonable. Preparing these standards before participating in the negotiating, and it will provide persuasive ammunition required in the negotiation.

Fairness or legitimacy is one of the most powerful of human motivations and thus constitutes a special category of interests. It routinely plays a major role in negotiation, too often (and unwisely) overlooked. It is not uncommon for negotiations to fail. A negotiation can fail not because the option on the table is unacceptable, but because it does not feel fair to one or both parties. In effect, people pay to avoid accepting a solution that feels illegitimate. Often this interest in legitimacy and feel fairly treated is the main driver in a dispute. Though parties with divergent views on what is fair may fail to realize that beneath their conflicting positions is the same interest.

When bargaining over positions, negotiators create a situation in which one side must concede his original claim in order for the negotiations to succeed. Positional bargaining is bargaining in which two sides lock into incompatible positions. This can lead to a contest of wills, bitterness and deadlock. They maintain that when negotiations are approached in this way, even when a deal is made, it may come at a high cost. For example, positional bargainers may finally arrive at a solution that appears to "split the difference" between their two positions, even though a more rationally composed solution would have suited both parties interests better. Lastly, agreements that are concluded in this manner may prove tenuous to implement if parties later conclude that the agreement called for a solution without legitimacy. The authors maintain that there is a better way to approach the negotiation process. This involves invoking objective criteria as part of the negotiation process.

Fair standards are markers outside of the parties to a conflict, for assigning some value to or for serving as the basis for a solution to a problem. The problem is not always so easily resolved because there may be multiple, potentially acceptable standards available from which to choose. For example, in our earlier illustration, should prices be based on market rates for similar products or domestic production costs? One party may maintain that a fair standard for determining the price of exported goods is the world market price. Another party may argue that a fair standard is the domestic price of the exported commodity in its country of origin. What other possible criteria can become the basis for a mutually acceptable fair standard? There are many. In negotiations of this type, parties often turn to arenas such as precedent, scientific judgement, professional standards, efficiency, costs, moral standards, equal treatment, tradition or reciprocity as plausible criteria for decision-making.

In negotiations, joint decision-making is a process that increases the perceived fairness of the negotiations, improves satisfaction with outcomes, promotes positive relations between parties, enhances the legitimacy with which agreements are viewed, and helps to create a willingness to abide by the commitments made. By framing negotiations as a decision-making process based upon objective criteria, negotiators free themselves and the other side from needing to cling to a position stubbornly in order not to appear weak or disingenuous. Whether negotiators chose fair standards or fair procedures, the essential point, according to the theory of principled negotiation is to jointly frame a sound basis for logical decision-making that both add value to the process. This, in turn, should ensure that parties can look back on the negotiated solution as a legitimate solution. Moreover, negotiations conducted in this manner become more efficient. Rather than spending their time attacking one another's positions, negotiators can focus their energies on analysis and problem-solving and stand a greater chance of crafting agreements that parties will view as legitimate as time goes on.

Communication

Without communication, there is no negotiation. Listen actively and acknowledge what is being said. Listening enables to understand their perception, feel their emotions and hear what they are trying to say. Ask the other party to spell out exactly what they mean or repeat ideas if they are unclear. Talk to the other side. Negotiation is not a debate! Have a clear dialogue. Describe a problem in terms of its impact rather than in terms of what happened

1. Listen actively to both verbal and non-verbal cues

2. Get beneath the surface – ask questions to learn

3. Describe the required "Data"

4. Inquire, don't try to persuade

Good communication can change attitudes, prevent or overcome deadlock and misunderstandings and help to improve relationships. Moreover, good communication skills are essential to cogently relay on the message and to thoroughly understand the message of the other side. In addition, integrative approaches stress the importance of sharing information as a means of uncovering interests and of helping parties to explore common problems or threats. Still, negotiators are frequently hampered in their roles by common communicational errors or inefficiencies. For example, parties may concentrate only on their own responses and forget to listen to what the other side is saying. Listening provides important information about the other side and demonstrates that being attentive to the other side's thoughts and respectful of their concerns.

Active listening is important to improve communication skills during negotiation. This means listening "not to phrase a response, but to understand the other party as they see themselves." Asking questions, paraphrasing without necessarily agreeing, and constantly acknowledging what is or is not said are good ways to demonstrate that to listening actively. Even when communication skills are good, communication problems can still arise.

Negative emotions can cloud a negotiator's ability to communicate effectively.

In addition, the existence of an audience to a negotiation – be it a constituency, a superior, or a mediator, can all influence communication style and efficiency. Many integrative theorists have emphasized the role of framing ineffective communications. As a communication tool, frames can help the other side to understand and relate to concerns about the requirement. Moreover, proper framing of a topic can promote a shared definition of a problem and the process needed to resolve the dispute. They maintain that by presenting the negotiations as a mutual problem to be solved together. Negotiators help to create a sense of ease, camaraderie and openness. In integrative approaches, framing is thus both a communication skill and a tool for improving the channels of communication.

Finally, negotiators should become attuned to the necessity of learning how to deal skillfully with difficult emotions which frequently arise in the course of negotiations. Allowing the other negotiator to release his or her feelings is an effective tactic for improving communication because it helps to clear the air of unwanted emotions and get talks back on track rather than let them be hung up on bad feelings. Thus, they recommend giving the other side the opportunity to let off steam when needed. If what the other party is feeling comes out in the form of verbal attacks or long and polemical speeches, they advise listening and being patient. Integrative theorists often stress the importance of confronting difficult emotions when they arise and making them explicit as a way of underscoring the seriousness of the problem, acknowledging their legitimacy, and making the negotiations more proactive. Negotiators should ask themselves how they would like to feel, and then ask the same questions from the perspective of the other side.

Relationship

The adage that people do business with people they like holds true in negotiation. Engaging in reasonable, principled negotiation will help to maintain a good relationship with the other side's negotiator. As that relationship grows in strength, it will be better able to negotiate with this person based on the store of goodwill that has been built.

The important variable in negotiation is the relationship a negotiator has or wants with other parties. This includes the negotiator's relationship both with those across the table and with anyone else who might affect the negotiation or be affected by the negotiator's reputation coming out of it. Having a fond or trusting relationship may make dispute resolution easier, while hostile feelings can make it much harder. Perhaps more importantly, the conduct and outcome of negotiation have the potential to either damage or strengthen a relationship in a variety of ways. As a result, the prospect of a dispute can be very stressful in an important ongoing relationship, such as that between a boss and an employee, or between sales and marketing. Sometimes, as with a family member or a business partner, maintaining a certain kind of relationship may be a much more important interest than the particular substantive issues in dispute. In other contexts, the parties may lack any personal or formal connection. But they nevertheless face the prospect of ongoing dealings, including occasional disputes, in which they would prefer to have a way of working things through that entails lower rather than higher transaction costs. However, even when there is neither a prior nor likely a future relationship with the other side, a negotiator still has to weigh the impact on the outcome of this negotiation of the working relationship between the parties during the negotiation. If that relationship becomes heated and hostile, the chances of agreement decline and the chances of a creative value-maximizing agreement decline precipitously. Finally, a negotiator also has an ongoing relationship with him or her that can influence the conduct of negotiation. Psychological drives to avoid inconsistency to preserve key values that define one's identity or to "do the right thing" may shape a negotiator's choices.

Commitment

Obviously, a successful negotiation closes with both sides committing to act on the negotiated settlement. However, commitments are important throughout a negotiation and start with a simple commitment to negotiate. As the sides work together to commit on the time and place of the negotiation, the manner of it and who can do what in the negotiation, they build positive momentum towards a final settlement.

A Circle Value Approach to Negotiation

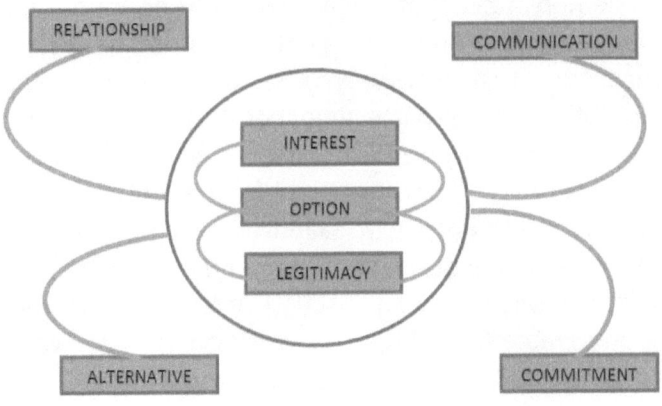

IF NO – IF YES

A negotiated settlement is only enduring if all parties honour the commitments that they make. Of course, those that fail to follow through on their promises stand to suffer a loss of integrity, be subject to the resentment of the other side and risk that their partner in the negotiations (and possibly others outside of the deal as well if word of their reputation escapes) will refuse to deal with them in the future. No party to negotiation should intentionally create commitments that they do not intend to honour. During the negotiating process, parties should think carefully about the kind of commitments they should be prepared to make. Are they capable of honouring them? How broad should the commitments be? When will each party be expected to make good on their promises? One way to build trust is to create a commitment structure that can be implemented in stages. Parties may be more willing to make a deal with an opponent when there is an opportunity to demonstrate that each side is honouring their commitments along the way. How can parties recover once the trust is broken? Gestures are one way through which a party who has lost integrity with another party due to past instances of actions in bad faith may begin to compensate for earlier grievances. For example, a party who failed to make the payment on a contractual obligation may need to offer advance payment on a new contract in order to convince a poorly treated trading partner that they are worth doing business with in the future.

7

IMPLEMENTATION

SOURCING DESIGN

A new structure of buying operation has to be designed based on the category. Grouping of the portfolio is highly essential in strategic sourcing implementation. The grouping is done based on the category and the codification that needs to be done. Separate codification should be given to all the categories. This will help us to monitor the consumption of commodities per month, and an annual understanding of the category is the first step in the process. This requires the collation of demand and usage information; locale, users as well as an understanding of the processes undertaken. Cross-functionally determining where and what to buy while minimising risk and costs. This could reveal single or multiple, make or buy activities to meet demand over the term. It is important to ensure stakeholders are part of the full process, including the final strategy signoff.

The Strategic Sourcing Model is based on a series of activities that must take place in order to be successful. Without following through all the necessary steps to discover where the spending trends are and where opportunities lie, we are simply purchasing in traditional ways. The final step in this process is to clearly identify the specifications for each item in that product category. If we are to leverage our spending and negotiate preferential contracts, then we better understand what exactly where we are buying.

The research, data analysis, specification development, and commodity classifications, determine the sourcing strategy and consolidated family products lines. It is ready to move into the bidding, supplier selection process and negotiations for a successful relationship. Successful strategic assessment will develop an understanding of the market. Strategic professionals will, therefore, understand the true importance of the supplier, the balance of supply and demand, new entrants into the marketplace, consolidations, alternatives, supplier capabilities, and overall strategic alliances. Once this is achieved, then the ultimate "Lowest Total Cost of Ownership" will be achieved. The package is put together for any specific commodity. It is time to send out for bidding. Today's electronic E-Commerce opens the door to a whole new world. The marketplace is no longer defined by geographic constraints.

The identification of suitable suppliers is as critical as any other step. You can negotiate the best price, delivery, payments terms, etc. But if the supplier isn't stable or in partnership, then what good will great pricing do for the company?

The following are suggestions for seeking out a suitable supplier:

1. Strong commitment to the environment, health and safety

2. Lean manufacturing and 5S principles are in place and visible

3. Cost competitive culture

4. Financially stable

5. Progressive management – clear and visible metrics

6. Understands and uses web-based paperless systems

7. Registered ISO or QS certifications

INCREASING THE STRATEGIC SOURCING REMIT

Increasing other value-adds of the purchasing and supply management function, i.e. not simply price reduction and penetrating aspects of the business which can be transformed into bought out expenditure, via outsourcing, for instance.

SOURCING PLANS

The preferred strategic sourcing options are agreed upon, and these are developed into 'sourcing plans' which should be innovative and creative solutions to the organisation's requirements in support of the organisation's mission and objectives. Strategic sourcing plans should generate workstreams, i.e. clear milestones to be achieved with resources. For example, project teams should be allocated appropriately. This is where the process of acquisition begins involving design teams, outcome-based specifications, market development, advertisements and policy compliance, for instance. Strategic sourcing plans include determining processes for tenderers, supplier selection and performance criteria for ensuring the supplier continues to meet customer's expectations.

IDENTIFYING NEW SUPPLIERS

Traditionally, sourcing has been perceived as the identification of new or alternative suppliers, e.g. sources of supply. Methods of identifying suppliers have included:

a. Internet, e.g. supplier's own pages and B2B trade bulletin boards

b. Trade associations and trade directories business supplier exhibitions

c. Networking with other buyers

d. Talking to specialist end-users. This process is now part of the strategic sourcing workstreams, i.e. only part of the sourcing process.

Select the Strategic Sourcing Process – choosing and using the various tools and methodologies are primary here. From simple manual or electronic Enquiry and Quote forms to formal PQQ's, RFI's, RFQ's, RFP's and e-Auctions are utilised here. The documents, processes and tools used can be hugely complex, split into numerous lots. The key is to ensure suppliers understand requirements and price it accordingly without it being overly onerous or lengthy. Product or service specifications, delivery and service requirements, pricing breakdown and legal and financial terms and conditions, as well as evaluation criteria, should be included here.

Following the development of strategic sourcing plans and the identification of workstreams, the purchasing and supply management function should facilitate the implementation of the strategic sourcing strategy. This may involve helping with or leading the contracting process, educating the internal customer or order placer; enabling the supplier, e.g. getting the supplier ready to deliver by developing and managing them etc.

In many larger organisations, the strategic sourcing part of purchasing and supply management is what purchasing and supply management professionals are primarily involved with. They are rapidly becoming less involved with the other aspects of contracting; i.e. purchasing and supply management to manage the less strategic and more straightforward aspects of purchasing and supply management.

MEASUREMENT

Strategic sourcing encompasses aspects of all of those activities and is not a replacement activity. Strategic sourcing is a skill set which must be put in practice, to be developed and refreshed. Strategic sourcing, as described in this policy, is becoming a common skill set for purchasing and supply management. It requires great resource and excellent management information and the organization should be in a position to implement it. It is a key element of the sourcing management process. It is the start of a continuous cycle, starting with benchmarking the current status, monitoring the results and ensuring that full value is being achieved. We should review the supply market again and restart the process in a constantly evolving marketplace.

These processes can be augmented with a range of core tools that include spend analysis, e-Sourcing, e-Auctions, Contract Authoring, Contract Management. Dependent on the size of the spend and knowledge and experience of the procurement team, categories can be globally or centrally managed, with regional and local procurement supporting as needed.

CLUSTER DEVELOPMENT

A cluster is a sectoral and geographical concentration of enterprises, i.e. micro, small and medium enterprises, manufacturing same or related products facing common opportunities and threats. Sectoral and geographical means the physical presence of a number of enterprises at one place or within a small radius say 8–10 kms. The clusters can give rise to the emergence of specialised suppliers of raw materials, machinery and spares, human skills, product-related services, etc.

The presence of the cluster gives way to create a conducive ground for the development of inter-firm cooperation and specialization as well as cooperation among public and private local institutions to further promote the sector. Although the critical mass or number of enterprises required for effective intervention may vary from cluster to cluster, the number of manufacturing/servicing enterprises in a cluster should not normally be less than 20.

The important objective of Cluster Interventions is to enhance the productivity and competitiveness through capacity building of the entrepreneurs and their businesses. Bridging the technological and operational gaps, and thus reducing the cost of production, improving quality of the products and worldwide benchmarking of the quality parameters, are the major value additions over multiple challenges in this space.

Industry clusters are groups of similar, related or homogenous companies in a defined geographic area that share common markets, technologies, worker skill needs, and which are often linked by buyer-seller relationships.

Clusters, however, do not involve and complete an industry or a sector. Clusters must not be equated to an Industrial Park.

Importance of Cluster

1. Common in the method of production, quality testing, water and energy conservation

2. Uniform and same kind of technology and marketing strategies

3. Active level of communication to all members

4. Common challenges and opportunities

5. Diagnostic study – emphasis on all aspects for the overall development of cluster

6. Forming Associations – trust-building and developing identity

7. Workshops, seminars, awareness campaigns, training and study visits

8. Common purchase at lower costs

9. Re-sourcing of better technology

10. Technology transfer through training/demonstrations

11. Apportion different aspects of production among units – leading to a specialization

12. Setting up of Common Facility Centre (CFC), Mini Tool Room, Testing Lab, Design Centre, Common Raw Material Bank

13. Common/complementary sales and branding

14. Easier Credit – use of Micro Finance/Credit Guarantee

15. Handholding support in general

VENDOR-MANAGED INVENTORY (VMI)

As replenishment frequencies play an important role in integrated inventory models to reduce the total cost of supply chains which many studies fail to model it in mathematical problems. Vendor-managed inventory (VMI) is a theory-based inspired by integration in supply chain management regarding system dynamics. In other words, it is known as Dynamic inventory method. This is the basis of bullwhip effort VMI in a family of business models in which the buyer of a product provides certain information to a supplier (vendor) of that product. The supplier takes full responsibility for maintaining an agreed inventory level. A third-party logistics provider can also be involved to make sure that the buyer has the required level of inventory by adjusting the demand and supply gaps.

This is one of the successful business models used by Walmart and big-box retailers. In this model, the risk has been shared, and customer inventory can be maintained by the supplier. Space and productivity increase and time-saving with cost benefits.

Layer Concept

In order to reduce the supplier base and grouping of components with sub-assembly wise layer concept has been developed. Tier – 1 Tier – 2 and Tier – 3 linked with each supplier for the supplies and quality and delivery. OEM will monitor the activities directly or indirectly to meet the requirement depending upon the job nature and requirement.

1. Minimum follow-up

2. Better Administration

3. Price monitoring

4. Quality and Readability

5. Ease to implement changes and innovation

6. Traceability

7. Inventory control

BENCH MARKING AND IMPLEMENTATION

Strategic sourcing is an approach to product procurement that continuously evaluates and re-assesses a company's purchasing behaviour in order to increase that company's profitability. Most large businesses have a buying strategy and know what they can spend, but many do not have an understanding of their data or a comprehensive strategic approach to sourcing.

Benefits of strategic sourcing go far beyond just a small cost savings

1. Price Analysis: Cost price of buying commodity can be monitored with respect to input material cost and operational efficiencies. The input raw material cost may escalate with a hike of taxes and global and local market trends and government policies.

2. Direct Material Cost (DMC): All the direct material cost in the product can be measured based on the category and spend analysis in the procurement. This can be altered and maintained the DMC with regular negations and changing sources and continuous improvement.

3. On-Time Delivery: This is one of the major subjects in the strategic sourcing right time

material is very important. Delayed material supplies will create a loss of time, production, money and customers. Every order delivery performance must be monitored and communicated to the supplier to maintain the OTD.

4. Quality: This is an important aspect of strategic sourcing. This process has to be jointly developed with an agreement of quality and testing procedure as per the quality and process plan.

5. Transportation: One of the key areas of money drain-out is transportation. This has to be fixed very clearly without any changing the cost. Pool system like a milk run to be employed for cluster collection and local collection of materials.

BIBLIOGRAPHY

1. Fisher, R. and Ury. W., 1981. *Getting to Yes: Negotiating Agreement Without Giving In.*: Penguin Books. New York, USA.

2. Gerd Kerkhoff et al.: *The Bermuda Triangle of Business* Wiley-VCH, Weinheim Düsseldorf 2005, ISBN 978-3-527-50123-6

3. Daniel Beimborn: *Cooperative sourcing: Simulation studies and empirical data on outsourcing coalitions in the banking industry.* Gabler, Wiesbaden 2008, ISBN 978-3-8350-0946-2

4. Payne, Joe and Dorn, William: *Managing Indirect Spend: Enhancing Profitability Through Strategic Sourcing* John Wiley & Sons, Inc., 2012, ISBN 978-0-470-88688-5

5. Nishiguchi, Toshihiro. *Strategic Industrial Sourcing* (New York: Oxford University, 1994) ISBN 0-19-507109-3

6. Payne, Joe and Dorn, William. *Managing Indirect Spend: Enhancing Profitability Through Strategic Sourcing* (John Wiley & Sons, Inc., 2012) ISBN 978-0-470-88688-5

7. Unpacking Competitive Bidding Methods: The Essential ABCs of the Various RFX Methods>[1]|2016|Vested Way|accessed 2 October 2016.

8. Nielsen Category Management – Positioning Your Organisation to Win,

9. Rationale for Category Management Archived 2008-03-06 at the Wayback Machine.

10. Fisher, R. and Ertel, D., 1995. *Getting Ready to Negotiate.*

11. Zartman, W.I., 1978. *The Negotiation Process: Theories and Applications.* Sage Publications Beverly Hills, California, USA.

12. Leigh Thompson, 'The Heart and Mind of the Negotiator-2nd Edition,' Prentice Hall Business Publishing, (2001).

13. J. Lewicki, A. Litterer, W. Minton, M. Sauders, 'Negotiation,' 2nd Edition, Irwin,(1994).

14. Raiffa, H., 2002. *Negotiation Analysis.* The Belknap Press of Harvard University Press. Cambridge & London, UK.

15. Odell, J.S., 2006. *Writing Negotiating Trade: Developing Countries in the WTO and NAFTA.* Cambridge University Press, New York, USA.

16. Walton, R.E. and McKersie, R.B., 1965. *A Behavioural Theory of Labour Negotiations: An Analysis of a Social Interaction System.* McGraw-Hill, New York, USA.

17. *D. Lax and J. Sebenius, The Manager as Negotiator (New York: Free Press, 1986).*

18. *Cohen, H. You can negotiate anything Angus & Robertson Sydney, 1990.*

19. *Andrea Schneider & Christopher Honeyman, eds., The Negotiator's Fieldbook, American Bar Association (2006). ISBN 1-59031-545-6 [4]*

20. *Leigh L. Thompson, The Mind and Heart of the Negotiator 3rd Ed., Prentice Hall Oct. 2005.*

21. *David Churchman, "Negotiation Tactics" University Press of America, Inc. 1993 ISBN 0-8191-9164-7*

22. *Shell, R.G. (2006). Bargaining for advantage. New York, NY: Penguin Books.*

23. *Roger Dawson, "Secrets of Power Negotiating – Inside Secrets from a Master Negotiator" Career Press, 1999.*

24. *Charles Arthur Willard. Argumentation and the Social Grounds of Knowledge University of Alabama Press. 1982.*

25. *Nicolas Iynedjian, Négociation – Guide pratique, CEDIDAC 62, Lausanne 2005, ISBN 2-88197-061-3*

26. *Michele J. Gelfand and Jeanne M. Brett, ed. "Handbook of negotiation and culture," 2004. ISBN 0-8047-4586-2*

27. *Howard Raiffa, The Art and Science of Negotiation, Belknap Press 1982, ISBN 0-674-04812-1*

28. *"Negotiating in bad faith," example of use of "bad faith" from definition in Oxford Online Dictionary.*

29. *UN Procurement Practitioner's Handbook – 2017.*